AWAKENING
GENIUS
IN • THE • CLASSROOM

Thomas Armstrong

ASCD

Association for Supervision and Curriculum Development
Alexandria, Virginia USA

Association for Supervision and Curriculum Development
1250 N. Pitt Street • Alexandria, Virginia 22314-1453
Telephone: 1-800-933-2723 or 703-549-9110 • Fax: 703-299-8631
On July 14, 1998, ASCD will move to new headquarters:
1703 N. Beauregard St., Alexandria, VA 22311-1714.
Telephone: 703-578-9600 • Fax: 703-575-5400.

Gene R. Carter, *Executive Director*
Michelle Terry, *Assistant Executive Director, Program Development*
Nancy Modrak, *Director, Publishing*
John O'Neil, *Acquisitions Manager*
Julie Houtz, *Managing Editor of Books*
Kathleen Florio, *Copy Editor*
Bob Land, *Proofreader*
Charles D. Halverson, *Project Assistant*
Gary Bloom, *Director, Editorial, Design, and Production Services*
Karen Monaco, *Senior Designer*
Tracey A. Smith, *Production Manager*
Dina Murray, *Production Coordinator*
John Franklin, *Production Coordinator*
Valerie Sprague, *Desktop Publisher*

ASCD publications present a variety of viewpoints. The views expressed or implied in this book should not be interpreted as official positions of the Association.

Printed in the United States of America.

July 1998 member book (pc). ASCD Premium, Comprehensive, and Regular members periodically receive ASCD books as part of their membership benefits. No. FY98-8.

ASCD Stock No.: 198033   ASCD member price: $8.95   nonmember price: $10.95

Library of Congress Cataloging-in-Publication Data
Armstrong, Thomas.
    Awakening genius in the classroom / Thomas Armstrong.
        p. cm.
    Includes bibliographical references.
    ISBN 0-87120-302-2 (pbk.)
    1. Learning, Psychology of. 2. Motivation in education. 3. Motivation (Psychology) in
children. 4. Cognitive styles. I. Title.
BF318 .A75 1998   98-19666
370.15'23—ddc21   CIP

03 02 01 00 99 98   10 9 8 7 6 5 4 3 2 1

AWAKENING GENIUS
IN THE CLASSROOM

Preface

I n an interview in the mid-1980s in a British psychology journal, Howard Gardner explained how he was being intentionally confrontational in his use of the term *intelligences* to form the basis for his renowned theory of multiple intelligences (Gardner 1983, 1993). Gardner remarked:

> I'm deliberately being somewhat provocative. If I'd said that there's seven kinds of competences, people would yawn and say "Yeah, yeah." But, by calling them "intelligences," I'm saying that we've tended to put on a pedestal one variety called intelligence, and there's actually a plurality of them . . . (Weinreich-Haste 1985, p. 48).

Gardner suggests here that by using a word that had been associated with high performances on standardized tests, he was able essentially to get people to wake up and pay attention to the importance of other ways of knowing.

In this book, I'd like to do something similar with the word *genius*. This word, even more than the word *intelligence*, has come to be associated with elite performances: scores of 130 or higher on I.Q. tests; extraordinary feats in music, art, and literature; and the very highest demonstrations of human competence in other domains as well. I recall a talk I gave in Berkeley, California, on "Awakening the Genius of Every Child" several years ago; a well-known East Coast sculptor in attendance became absolutely enraged at my use of the term *genius*. He felt that I was attempting to democratize a term that was clearly in his mind the province of only a very few rare individuals whose achievements he feared would be diluted by being thrown in with the masses in a sort of "Einstein Is Everyman" approach to learning.

It's not my intention in this book to argue that every child is an Einstein. There was only one Einstein. As you will see in Part 1, I am using the word *genius* in a much broader and deeper way, in a way that is actually much truer to its original meanings. As the reader begins this book, it will become apparent that I'm using the word *genius* in a way that closely links it to words such as *creativity*, *vitality*, *potential*, *motivation*, and *the joy of learning*. However, if I used those terms, people would just yawn and say, "Yeah, yeah. We've heard all that before." So, taking my cue from Dr. Gardner, I'm being deliberately provocative in choosing the word *genius*. And yet, just as Gardner's use of *intelligences* was perfectly appropriate for a discussion of other ways of knowing, so the word *genius* is a wonderful choice for a way to talk about that very deepest source of what drives the learning process in every child.

Part of what motivates me to write this book is a concern that we've lost touch in education with the sheer joy of what it means to learn something new. Observe a baby in the act of learning. You'll notice explosions of excitement, flailing of arms, bright eyes, and a kind of "dance of life." I'm troubled that modern educators have become so caught up in the world of standards, curriculum, assessment, discipline, management, budgets, politics, and bureaucracy that they have lost the ability to see clearly the simple truth of the joy of learning as the crucial foundation stone for everything else in learning. In his celebrated "rhythm of education" model, Whitehead (1932) describes three stages in learning: a period of *romance*, in which one celebrates the vitality and passion that accompany learning; a period of *precision*, in which one must commit sometimes substantial energy toward acquiring specific skills on the way to mastery of a subject; and a period of *generalization*, in which one directly applies this new learning to practical situations. As educators, we've spent almost all of our time focused on the last two stages and neglected the first stage: the romance of learning.

Recently, I did a computer search of the literature in ERIC (Educational Resources Information Clearinghouse) for citations related to the "joy of learning." Between 1982 and 1996 there were 13 "hits" and only two actual research studies related to the term. On the other hand, for "learning disabilities" there were 7,322 citations. This says a lot about priorities in educational research. I suspect that there might be an inverse relationship between these two sets of numbers. In other words, as we learn more about the joy of learning, we might have less need to find out about its agonies. It's my hope that *Awakening Genius in the Classroom* will provide new impetus for educators to make the inner genius of students and the joy of learning major research priorities for the new millennium.

Another reason that I decided to write this book is because of the overwhelming success of the theory of multiple intelligences over the past few years and my fear that its success could well keep educators from seeing its true significance. "Multiple intelligences" has become an educational slogan, joining "cooperative learning," "authentic assessment," "learning styles," and a number of other terms in education's latest group of buzzwords. Scores of books with lesson plans are now available (see, for example, Armstrong 1994, Bruetsch 1995, Campbell et al. 1996, Fogarty and Stoehr 1995, Haggerty 1995, Lazear 1991). So are checklists and formal and informal measures for assessing multiple intelligences (Bellanca et al. 1994, Shearer 1996, Teele 1992), posters and comic books on MI theory (Margulies 1995), videos (Gardner 1995, Armstrong 1997), audiotapes, and training programs. There is nothing wrong with the explosion in MI materials (I've quite liberally contributed to them myself). However, I fear that people will now relate to multiple intelligences in terms of these materials, seeing MI theory as a fad or a "thing" rather than as a deeper attitude toward honoring the different kinds of knowing that exist in our students.

I observe subtle signs of this "thingism" developing around the United States. I've seen hints of supervisors with evaluation sheets in hand going into classrooms expecting to see each of the intelligences used in a teacher's lesson plans. I've seen evidence of teachers and administrators using tests and checklists (mine included) to put kids into categories, like the "BK [bodily-kinesthetic] learner" or the "spatial kid," which can serve only to limit children's potentials rather than open them up. I've seen MI theory serve as new wine poured into old wineskins, with teachers simply relabeling the status quo using MI terms without changing anything at all in the way they teach, or merely introducing token activities ("Oh yes, I use MI . . . we do raps in math") without thinking about what really has to change in their fundamental attitudes about children, development, learning, school reform, and the ultimate purposes of education itself.

I hope that by going back to what I believe is the most fundamental issue in education—the intrinsic joy of learning or "genius" that every student possesses—I can re-emphasize why multiple intelligences has the potential to be so transformational in education and, at the same time, I can help remind teachers why most of us got into teaching in the first place. It certainly wasn't the money. And it probably wasn't to help children master page 24 of a phonics worksheet or to assist them in checking the correct answer on a standardized test. More likely it had something to do with getting kids excited about learning and helping them realize their fullest potential. I hope that this book will serve to awaken educators into thinking about multiple intelligences in a deeper way by reminding them why multiple intelligences was such a great idea when it first came out: because it provided a powerful language for describing the learning process in all of its richness and diversity. If multiple intelligences represents the rainbow of learning, then genius is the pot of gold at the end of the rainbow. I hope that *Awakening Genius in the Classroom* will reconnect you to an understanding of the "gold" that exists inside of each one of your students and that it will give you a living structure for making that rich treasure available to your students so that they can brighten the world around them.

EVERY STUDENT IS A GENIUS

Every student is a genius. I do not mean this in the psychometric sense of the word, in which an individual must score above the upper 99th percentile on a standardized measure of intelligence to qualify. Nor do I mean it in the sense of every student as a grandmaster chess champion, a virtuoso on the violin, or a world-class artist. These are some of the currently accepted meanings of the word *genius* in our culture and are not particularly relevant to the topic of this book.

For the meaning of *genius* used here, I have gone back to the origins of the word itself. According to the *Compact Oxford English Dictionary* (1991, p. 664), the word *genius* derives from Greek and Latin words meaning "to beget," "to be born," or "to come into being" (it is closely related to the word *genesis*). It is also linked to the word *genial*, which means, among other things, "festive," "conducive to growth," "enlivening," and "jovial." Combining these two sets of definitions comes closest to the meaning of the word *genius* used in this book: "giving birth to one's joy."

From the standpoint of education, *genius* means essentially "giving birth to the joy in learning." I'd like to suggest that this is the central task of all educators. It is the genius of the student that is the driving force behind all learning. Before educators take on any of the other important issues in learning, they must first have a thorough understanding of what lies at the core of each student's intrinsic motivation to learn, and that motivation originates in each student's genius.

The word *genius* has a rich multicultural history. The ancient Romans used it to refer to a guardian spirit that protected all individuals throughout their lives. All persons were born with their own unique genius that looked after them, helped them out of difficulties, and inspired them at crucial moments in their lives. On a person's birthday, the Romans would celebrate the birthday of the genius as well as the individual. The accomplishments of individuals were often attributed to their personal genius (*The New Encyclopaedia Britannica* 1980). In the Middle East, the term has been linked to the word *jinni*, or *genie*, that magical power chronicled in the *Arabian Nights* that lay dormant in Aladdin's lamp until a few rubs on the side of the vessel "gave birth" to a sometimes jovial and sometimes not so jovial spirit (Zipes 1991).

The genius is a symbol for an individual's potential: all that a person may be that lies locked inside during the early years of development. So, when we say as educators that we want to help students to develop their potential, we're essentially saying that we want to assist them in finding their inner genius and support them in guiding it into pathways that can lead to personal fulfillment and to the benefit of those around them.

The 12 Qualities of Genius

To provide a structure for educators that can make the concept of genius useful, I've expanded its meaning to include 12 basic qualities: curiosity, playfulness, imagination, creativity, wonder, wisdom, inventiveness, vitality, sensitivity, flexibility, humor, and joy. Unlike Gardner's eight intelligences (expanded from his original seven; see Gardner 1983, 1996), these 12 qualities are not based on any established criteria. The concept of genius could just as well be represented by 3 or 15 or 50 different qualities. However, the 12 qualities included here represent a wide selection of qualities that give structure to the somewhat elusive notion of genius. They are aspects of life that every educator has some familiarity with both inside and outside the classroom. And although these qualities may lack the rigorous application of criteria found in the theory of multiple intelligences (see Gardner 1983, pp. 59–70), they are supported, as we will see later, by research in the neurosciences, anthropology, developmental psychology, and other sources as well. Before sharing some of this research, however, I'd like to describe the 12 qualities that constitute the basic building blocks of each student's intrinsic genius.

Curiosity

Children are naturally curious about the world around them from the earliest weeks of life. The squirmy behavior of the infant is actually a manifestation of its sensorium engaged in a full-scale exploration of the world: this is active curiosity at its highest pitch. Once walking, the toddler moves toward whatever arouses curiosity. Once talking, the young child is constantly asking "Whazzat, mommy?" As the child grows into the elementary school years and acquires greater knowledge of the world, that curiosity branches out into hobbies, pastimes, collections, and interests that may change weekly. In adolescence, socially approved curiosity may weaken and be replaced by a more subterranean curiosity given over to the biggest questions about life, death, love, self, and truth.

The most curious thing is that often educators do not see the student's curiosity when it appears. Instead, they may regard it as "off-task" behavior, irrelevancies, silliness, and even rudeness. A teacher may be following a lesson plan on the American colonies when a student asks, "What's that necklace you're wearing made of?" In a behavior modification classroom that may result in a point off. At the very least it may throw a teacher off balance. An experienced teacher, however, knows how to take that question and make it serve the lesson plan's objectives ("It's made of shells. Do you think that some of the colonists might have worn shell necklaces?"). But more than using a child's curiosity to serve the needs of any particular lesson plan, educators need to recognize that these kinds of innocent questions emerge out of students' genius—their often insatiable need to find out everything they can about the world. Educators need to regard this curiosity as a healthy drive and not as an impediment to the smooth operation of their classroom. A major question should be how to take that intrinsic curiosity, in whatever form, and make it available to the curriculum (see Mann 1996).

Playfulness

Nowhere can we see students' genius more clearly demonstrated than when they are at play. When children play they reinvent the world. Kids who build forts and pretend to be kings and queens are internalizing social structures, mirroring historical movements, and playing out mythological themes. Play allows kids to work through emotional conflicts, develop and test hypotheses about the world, investigate complex social roles, prepare for full-fledged participation in the family and community, and develop more appropriate ways of relating to peers (see Singer 1973, Singer and Singer 1981). As the inventor of the kindergarten, Friedrich Froebel (1887), put it:

> Play is the highest level of child development. . . . It gives . . . joy, freedom, contentment, inner and outer rest, peace with the world. . . . The plays of childhood are the germinal leaves of all later life (pp. 54–55).

Playfulness, however, extends far beyond the kindergarten. It's really an attitude toward life that informs the behavior of the 4th grader who dances his way into the classroom as well as the playful manipulations of an 11th grade "wise guy." Teachers sometimes mistakenly think they're bringing play into the classroom by having kids play "games." Ironically, the formal rules and competitiveness of structured games often force playfulness into hiding. Playfulness is more likely to come up unexpectedly during the classroom day—for example, in the middle of a geometry lesson (the kid who starts walking around the room in a triangle pattern), while lining up to go to the lunchroom (the student who mimics the gruff lunchroom lady), or during sustained silent reading (the kids who create a "burping" symphony). When truly valued as an important component of students' genius, playfulness can find its way into many parts of the school day in an appropriate way (see, for example, Mann 1996).

Imagination

It's almost a cliché that children have vivid imaginations. A Gary Larson cartoon portrays this humorously by showing a mother entering her son's bedroom, with the boy cowering in bed. The mother exclaims, "How can you tell me there's a monster in this room when you can't even describe his face to me!" And in the corner of the room, a monster stands with a bag over his head!

Very young children are often terrified in the middle of the night because their dreams (and nightmares) appear as real as outer perceptions. Scientists call this facility "eidetic imagery," and some research suggests that this capacity exists to a far greater extent in childhood than in adulthood (see McKim 1980, p. 95). Children and adolescents can close their eyes and see all sorts of images: swirls of color, cartoon pictures, video-like images of places they'd rather be, and, in particular, stories and fantasies of wishes and dreams. Children and adolescents are constantly telling themselves stories in their heads, perhaps heroic sagas in which they play the hero or heroine, or space-age odysseys gleaned from *Star Wars* movies, or monster truck races in which they outpace the field, or turgid romances of loves lost and gained. All this may go on while the teacher is talking about the times tables or the Treaty of Versailles. In terms of sheer entertainment value, the Treaty of Versailles generally loses out against these personalized dramas! The imagination has come to be associated with something negative—daydreaming—rather than being viewed as a potential source of cognitive power that the student might use to write stories (e.g., "My Role in Writing the Treaty of Versailles"), put on plays, create works of art, initiate deep dialogues about significant life issues, or engage in other activities that relate to important school outcomes (see, for example, Samples 1976, Egan 1992, Litterst and Bassey 1993, Greene 1995).

Creativity

The word *creativity* is closely linked to the word *genius*, since both words have the root meaning "to give birth." Essentially, *creativity* designates the capacity to give birth to new ways of looking at things, the ability to make novel connections between disparate things, and the knack for seeing things that might be missed by the typical way of viewing life. Children and adolescents, being relatively new to life, are naturally creative because they haven't been brainwashed, so to speak, by the conventional attitudes of society. Consequently, students are always coming up with novel images, words, and actions that may delight, enlighten, or inspire adults. Composer and conductor Leonard Bernstein once declared that all music is derived from a basic melody that children throughout the world use in their own self-created songs and chants (Gardner 1981), and Chernoff (1979) related how Dagomba children from Ghana create social and political songs that have a direct influence on the culture. Russian writer Kornei Chukovskii (1963) once declared that young children were linguistic geniuses because of their ability to come up with creative expressions, and Bickerton (1982) suggested that children had created an entire creole language in Hawaii in the last century through the intermingling of many peoples and languages.

In the classroom, this creativity manifests itself in the poems, drawings, novel observations, and unique expressions that pour out of children at irregular times during the school day. It is apparent, for example, in Maria, a 3rd grader who writes: "I used to have a teacher of meanness/But now I have a teacher of roses" (Koch 1970, p. 14); in Alex, a 1st grade "bad boy" who moves like a flamenco dancer (Gallas 1994, p. 57); or in Don, the 10th grader who, an art teacher once told me, could turn any piece of solid wood into a human face. Creativity has not been the subject of intense focus, extensive research, or high levels of funding in American education. Typically, educators have relegated the topic of creativity to gifted education, and research in creativity has been used to identify children for admittance into gifted programs (see, for example, Getzels and Jackson 1962, Gowan et al. 1967, Torrance 1962, Renzulli 1986). But by limiting creativity to gifted education, educators have effectively isolated it from the mainstream of American education where it could do the most good. Creativity is a part of every student's birthright, and by recognizing it as such, we can make a good start in bringing it to the fore in every classroom (see, for example, Israel 1995, Hunter 1993).

Wonder

Wonder is the natural astonishment that children and adolescents have about the world around them. Most of us, at one time or another in our youth, have lain on our backs looking up at the sky on a starry night wondering how far the universe went on. This kind of experience reveals the dual meaning of wonder: as a verb ("I wonder how far it goes on") and as an emotional experience ("Wow! It just goes on and on . . . !"). It also underlies something particularly profound about the learning process that receives virtually no attention in education: those learning experiences that have the greatest impact on students are often those that involve awe or wonder. Such experiences emerge almost incidentally in the classroom when, for example, a student first encounters a blossom opening up in a classroom biology experiment, or sees a prism breaking light up into the colors of the rainbow, or experiences a particularly moving play or musical piece.

Wonder doesn't show up as a "skill" on any competency checklist—and thank goodness it doesn't; for by measuring some things we destroy them. But wonder nevertheless is a component of genius that both reveals the depths of our students' minds and deepens the learning process whenever it occurs. To reduce wonder to an "experience of affect" puts it on a level with those momentary cheap thrills that popular culture seems to thrive on. The experience of wonder is an encounter with the mysteries of life, and our students are particularly well equipped as natural geniuses to revel in this way of encountering the world (see Harwood 1958, Lorie 1989).

Wisdom

Out of wonder may come wisdom. The student who is able to experience the wonder of the world directly, without the blinders of preconceptions and clichés, has access to a certain precocious wisdom different from that of elders who have acquired their wisdom from years of experience; but this strong and silent knowledge nevertheless can have the force of deeper truth behind it.

Wisdom expresses itself in many ways. The 1st grader who draws a globe and a rainbow image during art class and says quietly that it stands for world peace is revealing a certain kind of wisdom. So too is the high school junior who writes an impassioned philosophical treatise on the nature of human goodness as a civics assignment. Wisdom may come across in a simple comment made during recess to help a younger child feel better or in a child's particularly sensitive intervention to help resolve a classroom conflict.

Robert Coles (1967, 1986a, 1986b, 1990) has done a particularly good job of revealing wisdom in children by documenting their struggles with poverty and discrimination as well as by revealing their deeper thoughts about religion, politics, morality, and other basic life issues (see also Armstrong 1984, Silverstein 1980, Wickes 1966). Like so many other qualities of genius described in this book, wisdom has not been given much credence by educators as a trait worth studying in the classroom (though a teacher may give it value by saying about a particular student, "That child is wise beyond his years"). However, along with Coles's work, there is a body of research (Matthews 1980, 1984, 1994; Lipman et al. 1980) suggesting that real wisdom and philosophical understanding exist in children and adolescents and are worth paying attention to as an educational resource.

Inventiveness

Though closely allied to the concept of creativity, inventiveness is included here as a separate dimension of genius because it implies a certain "hands-on" quality that might be neglected when people think about creativity. Children and adolescents are naturally inventive, coming up with often bizarre and funny uses for common things. I'm reminded of the 1st grade student who drew an image of a boy with peanuts pouring into his head (the top half of which was conveniently hinged to allow for this); the peanuts were ground together inside of his brain and blended with butter in a tube to make peanut butter, which he then sold door to door on his skateboard (Armstrong 1987a). Kids are always having these kinds of zany thoughts, which we're likely to dismiss out of hand without marveling at their truly geniuslike nature. It takes something rather extraordinary to turn an empty milk carton into an "owl car wash," or to design a Rube Goldberg–type device that moves ping-pong balls into sockets, causing bells to ring and a miniature pig to spin around, thus moving an alligator's head that functions as a pencil sharpener (Houston 1982). But students generally have little time to exercise their "inventive" muscles because educators may fear such amusing side trips of the mind take valuable time away from the core curriculum. Inventiveness should be seen as a *part* of the core curriculum—as part of a genius curriculum than can allow kids to contribute their cognitive fancies to whatever is being studied and thereby immeasurably enrich the experience of learning.

Vitality

Other words I might have chosen to express this dimension include *aliveness, spontaneity,* or *vibrancy.* But *vitality* seems to best express the image of children or adolescents being awake to their senses, totally and immediately responsive to the environment, and actively engaged in each and every moment. This dimension should not be confused with *impulsivity,* which has a certain driven or automatic quality reflected in unconscious and irritating behaviors. The vitality of the child or adolescent has a definite positive quality, though it might be judged as irritating if the environment around the student is dead. Vitality is really the essential spark of genius; the direct energy of the life force surging up into the world and making a direct impact (some teachers might say a "direct hit") on the classroom atmosphere. It's the enthusiasm of a kindergartner who has something special to share for show-and-tell. It's the high-energy demonstration of a science fair project by a 4th grade girl. It's the electric performance of a high school senior portraying Puck in Shakespeare's *A Midsummer Night's Dream*.

Sometimes teachers worry about containing this vitality in the classroom, believing that the best classroom is a subdued classroom. And at times, this vitality may verge on chaos. But at such times, it may be important for teachers to remember Nietzsche's comment: "One must have chaos within to give birth to a dancing star"; and Ashton-Warner (1986), who spoke of "organic chaos" in her definition of a creative learning atmosphere. The truly brilliant moments of teaching and learning are those in which deadness dies and vitality reigns supreme.

Sensitivity

This quality of genius refers to the incredible openness that children have to the world. From the earliest days of life, the sights, sounds, textures, smells, and tastes of the world flood the baby's sensorium, and the infant responds to each stimulus in a fresh and unique way. Although children and adolescents develop defenses as they grow to shield themselves from the more painful onslaughts that the world delivers, they are still highly sensitive to the experience of life compared to many of the adults around them who have erected walls to keep much of life safely outside. Sometimes the child's or adolescent's openness is regarded in a negative way, as "vulnerability," and the word *sensitivity* itself is often considered a deficit term (as in "you're just being too sensitive"); however, in the context of the qualities of genius described here, sensitivity is a clear asset that enriches the experience of life by making it more vivid. The child who cries after reading a sad novel is having a richer experience of the work than one who simply derives a purely intellectual knowledge of the plot. The student who becomes incensed when a teacher's opinion on pollution contrasts with his own can use his sensitivity to engage more intensively in the dialogue. The sensitivity of children and adolescents allows them to be more deeply affected by great works of art, music, dance, and literature, and to be moved by the events of history and the discoveries of science and math. Educators must respect this sensitivity, for its misuse and abuse can lead to subtle forms of brainwashing, to emotional scars from being exposed to inappropriate learning techniques, or to being led astray by poor role models. However, when wisely and delicately handled, the sensitivity of children and adolescents serves as a keystone to learning at its best.

Flexibility

This quality of genius refers to the plasticity of the child's (and to a lesser extent the adolescent's) mind; the ability of the child and adolescent to make fluid associations, to move from fantasy to reality, from metaphor to fact, from the inner world to the outer and back again. Like so many of the qualities of genius described earlier, this trait is often regarded as a liability. Child development texts report that as children grow up they must learn to distinguish fantasy from reality. This is quite correct and highly desirable as far as coping with the demands of the outer world. However, there is also an advantage to being able to move voluntarily between the worlds of fantasy and reality, or between other kinds of worlds—social, imaginal, physical, artistic, intellectual, and more. In such flexible journeys one can find the roots of culture itself. Children seem to have this ability to go on such fantastic voyages—for example, moving from a discussion about a bruise on the head, to thinking about what a bruise on an insect's head might feel like, to wondering whether insects have their own hospitals, to planning an "insect emergency room" as a class project.

Teachers who think in inflexible ways (as in "This learning event must relate to instructional objective x, y, or z") are likely to be stymied by this kind of thinking, and yet it is used in one of the oldest and most revered approaches to learning—the ancient art of storytelling—and also in one of the newest and most cutting-edge ways of processing information—hypertext language in computer software, which seems to branch out from one subject or topic to a multiplicity of ideas. By honoring the flexibility of the child or adolescent mind, educators can help students explore a broader expanse of knowledge than is possible through the more conventional "chunk-by-chunk" style of learning.

Humor

Many people have asked me during my workshops on multiple intelligences whether humor is an intelligence. I don't believe that it qualifies as an intelligence under Gardner's criteria (Gardner 1983), but I certainly feel there is something quite special about humor that deserves recognition. It seems very compatible with the other qualities of genius; for humor is a trait that, like creativity, breaks out of ruts and routines and causes a crackle of excitement or aliveness to occur in a group of people. Humor lifts us out of the dreadful seriousness of nongenius life, breaks the tension that drudgery all too often fixes upon us, and gives us something new: a funny angle, a new perspective, a broader view of life.

The genius preschooler seems to be always finding things in life to be amused by. In the classroom, a student's sense of humor may often seem to the teacher to be a distraction from the serious business of learning. However, humor should more appropriately be viewed as evidence of a different kind of mind at work. Humor can emerge anywhere around the curriculum: in a funny pun or limerick, a whimsical cartoon or drawing, the ludicrous gait of a character in a Shakespearean comedy, or even in a humorous answer to a math problem ("But Mrs.

Jones, 2 plus 2 must equal 5 in *some* alien's math system!"). Recent research has linked humor to health (Cousins 1979), and educational research has shown that it promotes learning on a number of different levels (see Hebert 1991). It's time educators gave humor more than just a fool's place in the curriculum.

Joy

If genius has any core component, it is probably the experience of joy. Ask some of the great minds of our time to explain what motivates them in their work and generally you will not hear them talk about pay checks or even the Nobel Prize (though these certainly have their allure). More often they may speak somewhat mystically of an experience that sounds like joy. Young children may not be as articulate, but if they could speak about what motivates them in their most passionate play experiences they would probably speak of joy (they speak of it anyway through their sparkling eyes, their bouncing bodies, and their squeals of delight). As Piaget (1975) once wrote: "On seeing a baby joyfully watching the movements of his feet, one has the impression of the joy felt by a god in directing from a distance the movement of the stars" (p. 153).

Joy is something mysterious that cooks up from deep inside of us when a new connection has been made, a new insight obtained, a new feat accomplished, or a skill mastered. Such joy can be witnessed in the brilliant grin of a high school student who witnesses the invention that he's been toiling on for the past several weeks finally work for the first time. Joy is in the 7th grader who twirls across the stage in the school musical. Joy shows itself in the 1st grader who jumps up and down after reading his first story. The neurochemistry of the joy of learning is still unclear—it might have something to do with neuronal connections stimulating a release of neuropeptides into the nervous system. But however it occurs, its importance cannot be underestimated. Without joy, learning is like soda pop without the fizzle—flat and tasteless (see Leonard 1968, Kline 1988, Sornson and Scott 1997).

Theoretical Foundations

The kinds of qualities described above have always been seen as belonging to the most endearing aspects of childhood. They've been romanticized by poets and lyricized in cute and cuddly songs about children. In education, they've been associated with the more humanistic, or "warm and fuzzy," wing of teaching and learning (see, for example, Canfield and Wells 1976). However, it's important to emphasize at this point that these qualities of genius are as significant and as real as other concepts— such as problem-solving ability, social skills, and learning styles—that are held in higher regard and that are more heavily researched by mainstream educators. The following sections present an initial theoretical basis for these 12 qualities of genius. Researchers and practitioners alike can use this information to further investigate the validity of these (or similar) characteristics both inside and outside the classroom. The theoretical basis encompasses four perspectives: neurological, evolutionary, biographical, and phenomenological.

Neurological Basis

The qualities of genius that I've enumerated are not associated with specific brain regions in the same way as are the intelligences in Gardner's theory of multiple intelligences (Gardner 1983, 1996). However, a body of literature does exist that has examined the neurological substrates of certain positive emotions that might be associated with some of the qualities, such as joy, humor, and curiosity (see, for example, Davidson 1992, 1994; Ekman and Davidson 1993). Looking more globally at brain development, it is worth noting that the infant brain has more *synaptic connections* (linkages between neurons) than an adult brain. As Gardner (1983) writes:

> In human beings, the density of synapses increases sharply during the
> first months of life, reaches a maximum at the ages of one to two
> (roughly 50 percent above the adult mean density), declines between
> the ages of two and sixteen, and then remains relatively constant until
> the age of seventy-two. More than one scientist has speculated that
> the extremely rapid learning of the young child (for example, in the
> area of language) may reflect an exploitation of the larger number of
> synapses available at that time (pp. 44–45).

This early proliferation of synapses suggests a certain geniuslike capacity
in the very young child (taking genius in the broader sense used in this
book).

To be sure, researchers have postulated more prosaic reasons for both
the rapid increase and the subsequent selective death of synaptic connections as the child grows. Nature seems to have built in redundancies
so that if some synaptic connections are damaged others will remain to
provide the necessary functions. Synapses also appear to compete with
one another for functional positions in true Darwinian fashion, with the
survival of the fittest ensuring that only the hardiest *dendrites* (the parts
of a nerve cell that receive messages) will form a permanent part of the
brain's structure (see Cowan 1979). To a certain extent, then, the
"pruning," or selective cell death, that occurs from ages 2 to 16 is an
inevitable part of nature's "spring cleaning" operation.

However, the question of the young child's neurologically rich
endowment, and its subsequent decline, takes on greater significance for
educators when we consider the important role of the environment in
shaping the child's brain. From experiments with laboratory animals we
now know that dendrite density can be either increased or decreased
depending upon the kinds of experiences provided. Laboratory rats in
an enriched learning environment (cages with mazes and running

wheels) have larger synaptic junctions in their brains than rats in "impoverished" cages (those without any accessories) (Rosensweig et al. 1972, Diamond 1988). Monkeys that have had one eye sutured shut during a critical period of optical cell development in the brain end up with fewer cells in the areas of the visual cortex responsible for processing information from that eye (Cowan 1979). To a certain extent, then, the kind of brain that develops to maturity depends upon the types of experiences the brain has undergone (see Sylwester 1995).

It seems reasonable to speculate that just as the absence of speech sounds in the environment may starve verbal connections in the brain (see, for example, Blakeslee, August 1, 1997), so, too, the absence of role models in a child's environment that display characteristics of some or all of the 12 qualities of genius may starve dendrites in those portions of the brain that support these behaviors. Thus, although much of the selective cell death or "pruning" that occurs in the child from ages 2 to 16 may still be "spring cleaning," which connections are actually pruned and which remain, as far as the qualities of genius in this book are concerned, may depend upon what is present or absent in the environment. An environment that fails to recognize the importance of the 12 qualities of genius may starve those traits out of existence, while surroundings that are "genius friendly" may well create neurological connections that facilitate their growth.

Evolutionary Basis

The flexibility of the human brain appears to have come about for very good evolutionary reasons. If human beings were born with a brain that was already hard-wired in every respect to respond to the environment in a fixed and unalterable way, we'd probably be extinct. A key to the survival of species is the ability to adapt to environmental changes. One reason that we have managed to survive and thrive as a species is because our brain is capable of adapting to a wide range of environments—in fact, our brain has the ability to wait until it directly experiences a specific environment and then program itself to function within just that setting (assuming the environment isn't too hostile). This un-committedness confers tremendous evolutionary advantages on human beings over other organisms that have far less neurological flexibility.

Such biological advantages become even more apparent when we look at a key evolutionary concept called *neoteny*. Neoteny literally means "holding youth" and refers to the process by which youthful traits in a species are retained into adulthood. One of the best illustrations of this can be seen by looking at the forehead and jaw structures of an infant and adult chimpanzee. In the infant, the broad forehead and rounded jaw appear very humanlike. In the adult, these humanlike features are gone: the forehead virtually disappears behind the bony eye sockets, and the jaw juts out into space beyond the nose and eyes. With respect to these two physical traits, neoteny does not exist in the chimpanzee; the childhood jaw and forehead are *not* retained into adulthood. In *Homo sapiens*, however, the child's jaw and forehead resemble those of the adult in their overall shape. In this case, neoteny *does* apply: the youthful traits *are* held or kept as the child grows into maturity. Gould (1977) points out that

> the theory of human neoteny is now usually relegated to a paragraph or two in anthropology textbooks. Yet I believe that it is fundamen-tally correct: an essential, if not dominant, theme in human evolution (p. 66).

The principle of neoteny becomes especially relevant to our discus-sion of the qualities of childhood and adolescent genius when we look, not at physical traits, but at psychological ones. Montagu (1983) sug-gests that there are 26 neotenous drives in children, including nine of the dimensions of genius listed above: sensitivity, curiosity, playfulness, imagination, creativity, flexibility, joy, humor, and wonder (Montagu's list was instrumental in helping to generate the qualities of genius in this book). He suggests that these neotenous characteristics represent important traits that are crucial to the further evolution of the human species. Montagu writes:

> From their "mature adult" heights adults only too frequently look down patronizingly upon the "childish" qualities of the child, without any understanding of their real meaning. Such adults fail to understand that those "childish" qualities constitute the most valuable possessions of our species, to be cherished, nurtured, and cultivated (pp. 196–197).

If our civilization is to keep from blowing itself off the map, we need to cultivate in our educational system people with the curiosity, sensitivity, and imagination, among other qualities, to come up with new ways of preventing wars, disease, and overpopulation. Montagu's perspective suggests that the qualities of genius, far from being "warm fuzzy" concepts, are the basic building blocks of humanity's hope for survival.

Biographical Basis

One of the best ways to study the role of neoteny in helping to effect transformation in civilization is to examine the lives of adults who are officially acknowledged to be geniuses in every sense of the word. Such an investigation reveals that many "official geniuses" possess qualities that are very much like the qualities of student genius described earlier. If any one person in our century were to be deemed a genius, it would probably be Albert Einstein. Posters of his likeness grace many classrooms as a symbol of towering intellect. Reflecting on his slow development in learning to speak, Einstein said,

> I sometimes ask myself . . . how did it come that I was the one to develop the theory of relativity. The reason, I think, is that a normal

adult never stops to think about problems of space and time. These are things which he has thought of as a child. But my intellectual development was retarded, as a result of which I began to wonder about space and time only when I had already grown up. Naturally, I could go deeper into the problem than a child with normal abilities (Clark 1984, pp. 27–28).

Einstein brought a childlike disposition toward looking at space and time into his powerful adult mind (a wonderful example of neoteny), and our view of the universe was never again the same.

Examples abound of childlike qualities serving a central role in the problem-solving capacities of extraordinary individuals. Sir Alexander Fleming, the Scottish bacteriologist who discovered penicillin, was very playful in his scientific investigations. He created little pictures of ballerinas and houses in petri dishes by using his knowledge of the colors and growth rates of different microorganisms. "I play with microbes," commented Fleming. "It is very pleasant to break the rules" (Cole 1988). Pablo Picasso wrote, "I used to draw like Raphael, but it has taken me a whole lifetime to learn to draw like a child." Henri Matisse declared, "I shall like to recapture that freshness of vision which is characteristic of extreme youth, when all the world is new to it." Even Shakespeare had childlike qualities of curiosity and whimsical fancy that penetrated his timeless plays, much to the chagrin of more serious literary types such as Dr. Samuel Johnson, who wrote, "A quibble is to Shakespeare what luminous vapors are to the traveler; he follows it at all adventures; it is sure to lead him out of his way and sure to engulf him in the mire" (quoted in Wright and Lamar 1964, p. xi).

To be sure, I am not saying that extraordinary individuals think like children and adolescents. One should never confuse the paintings of a five-year-old with the childlike simplicity of a painting by Miró or Chagall, nor a 2nd grader's simple musings on the size of the universe with Einstein's formal scientific papers on the theory of relativity.

However, it appears that many (if not most) extraordinary individuals possess attitudes of mind that are very similar to those of children and adolescents, and that when added to their formal training, years of effort, and unique capacity for synthesis, lead to transformative works. These attitudes of mind—or qualities of genius, as I've chosen to call them—may be as essential to the ultimate success of many extraordinary individuals as other factors in their biographies, and perhaps even more so. It was, after all, Einstein who was famous for the saying: "The imagination is everything." Having their origins in childhood, such qualities of extraordinary people need to be given special value by educators when they occur in the lives of so-called ordinary children and adolescents.

Phenomenological Basis

A fourth foundation stone for the 12 qualities of genius emerges from research studies documenting how individuals in the act of learning something new directly experience these qualities. Such research must be phenomenological or experiential by nature because quantitative methods such as checklists or tests can never capture the spirit or essence of these qualities. Literature in this area does exist and in fact thrives in many parts of education and psychology. However, it remains for practitioners and researchers to collect and frame these experiences into an organized body of work that reflects the 12 qualities of genius or some similar framework.

A number of anecdotal accounts provide examples of how the dimensions of genius are expressed. Piaget's work certainly bears mention since his careful observations of children and adolescents, beginning with his own offspring, hold a central place in the literature of child development and education. In one observation of his infant son Laurent's crib explorations, Piaget (1952) writes:

> Laurent, by chance, strikes the chain while sucking his fingers. He grasps it and slowly displaces it while looking at the rattles. He then begins to swing it very gently, which produces a slight movement of the hanging rattles and an as yet faint sound inside them. Laurent then definitely increases by degrees his own movements. He shakes the chain more and more vigorously and laughs uproariously at the result obtained (p. 185).

Although Piaget appeared more concerned with the cognitive dimensions of this type of behavior (using it as an example of early hypothesis testing, for example), this anecdote clearly describes aspects of curiosity, playfulness, and vitality. It is, in fact, these types of qualities that give the learning experience its special vibrancy.

A rich source of material for investigating the genius qualities of childhood exists in those early recollections of adults remembering the most momentous learning events in their lives. Perhaps the most famous example is Helen Keller's discovery of language at the water pump. According to Keller's own account,

> As the cool stream gushed over one hand, she [Annie Sullivan] spelled into the other the word water, first slowly, then rapidly. I stood still, my whole attention fixed upon the motions of her fingers. Suddenly I felt a misty consciousness as of something forgotten—a thrill of returning thought; and somehow the mystery of language was revealed to me. I knew then that W-A-T-E-R meant the wonderful cool something that was flowing over my hand. . . . I left the well-house eager to learn. Everything had a name, and each name gave birth to a new thought. As we returned to the house every object which I touched seemed to quiver with life (quoted in Lash 1980, p. 55).

Another example from Piaget is his recounting of the memories of a mathematician friend learning about number theory as a five-year-old:

> He was seated on the ground in his garden and he was counting pebbles. Now to count these pebbles he put them in a row and he

counted them one, two, three up to ten. Then he finished counting them and started to count them in the other direction. He began by the end and once again found he had ten. He found this marvelous. . . . So he put them in a circle and counted them that way and found ten once again (quoted in Ginsburg and Opper 1969, p. 170).

Walters and Gardner (1986), following Feldman (1980), call great learning moments that seem to propel individuals toward their destinies "crystallizing experiences," and they provide many additional examples, including Renoir's spellbinding encounter with a 16th-century sculpture at the age of 12, and Wagner's attendance at a performance of Beethoven's opera *Fidelio*, after which he wrote a letter to the lead singer dedicating his life to music and then "ran out into the street, quite mad."

It's important to remember that such genius experiences are not just the province of the recognized geniuses in society; they occur in the lives of so-called ordinary people as well. In one study conducted at Manchester College in Oxford, England (Robinson 1983), a 50-year-old woman vividly recalled being a child of 3 or 4 learning about the properties of space for the first time:

We were walking home along the pavement. I became spontaneously aware that each step I took decreased the way between me and my point of departure. I had no sufficient command of language to tell anyone. It was perhaps the most thrilling and significant thing that has ever happened to me. There was something there to do with perfection, a perfect conjunction of increasing and decreasing. . . . And when I was 15, the formulation came, in a history lesson, and I let out a great shout of joy, and was duly reprimanded (p. 112).

In another example from the study, an adult reported a sudden insight at the age of 7 while attending a grammar lesson in school:

I had an extraordinarily vivid insight which is absolutely beyond description but which has remained with me ever since as an abiding spiritual experience. The teacher was explaining that in addition to common nouns and proper nouns there were also abstract nouns, which mostly ended in "-ness," such as goodness, badness, etc.; also a number of short but very important words such as love, hate, etc. It was at this point that I seemed to grow up mentally (pp. 27–28).

These type of ecstatic learning experiences are akin to the "aha!" or "Eureka!" moments in the creative process (see Ghiselin 1955, Harman and Rheingold 1984). They also appear to share certain characteristics with the concept of "flow" as described in Csikszentmihalyi (1990). Through extensive interviews with highly accomplished adults in a number of fields including medicine, rock climbing, and the arts, Csikszentmihalyi discovered that people in radically different disciplines often describe the same sort of experience when particularly absorbed in their work. They seem to enter a state of mind that is totally awake and totally focused on the task, and yet detached from the activity such that the distinctions between doer and deed disappear, replaced by a spontaneous experience that is almost like a moving meditation. Csikszentmihalyi reports that children "have flow states all the time" (Begley 1986).

The concept of flow, in fact, bears a striking resemblance to Montessori's description of "the great work," her term for transformative moments when children become totally absorbed in the learning process. In one description of a three-year-old girl intent on placing cylinders of different widths into their respective containers—like corks in a bottle—Montessori (1973) reported the girl being so focused on her work that she remained undisturbed even when Montessori tested her concentration by picking her up in her chair and placing her on a small table. The girl moved the materials onto her knees and continued working without missing a beat. Montessori observed:

Then she stopped as if coming out of a dream and smiled happily. Her eyes shone brightly and she looked about. She had not even noticed what we had done to disturb her. . . . Similar events kept recurring, and every time children emerged from such an experience, they were like individuals who had rested. They were filled with life, and resembled those who have experienced some great joy (p. 119).

Montessori regarded this kind of event with a sense of sacred awe and saw it as the heart of the learning experience.

* * *

There appears, then, to be substantial evidence for both the existence and the significance of the kinds of genius qualities described earlier. Traditionally, these qualities have been given lip service by educators who mention them at the beginning of the school year to inspire teachers in bringing out the best in their students. Unfortunately, these qualities tend to become severely undervalued once the routine of the school year gets underway and other matters—such as instructional objectives, standards, and discipline—take center stage. The material presented here, however, suggests that these 12 qualities of genius (or similar qualities) need to be taken very seriously by educators throughout the school year. Educational researchers need to give more attention to documenting these qualities and describing the conditions that can best facilitate their daily presence in the classroom. In courses on teaching methods (as well as through inservice workshops), teachers need to re-value these qualities as core educational concepts and learn practical ways of making them happen more often in their classrooms. By regarding the genius of students as a solid reality—not as a fluffy metaphor—educators can effect perhaps the greatest transformation ever seen in our schools.

For Further Study

1. Describe any of the 12 qualities of genius in specific students that you've worked with in an educational setting. How could you best document those qualities (e.g., through a teacher journal, video or audio tape, student work, etc.)? Discuss individual students and their genius qualities with colleagues.

2. Describe times during the school day when special insights, joyful connections, experiences of ecstatic learning, "flow" states, or other peak moments of learning have taken place among your students. Share these experiences with your colleagues.

3. Discuss with your colleagues the extent to which your school or school district values the 12 qualities of genius (or similar qualities). Which of the 12 are particularly valued and which are especially undervalued?

4. Recollect times in your own childhood when you experienced special moments of learning something new. Recall, if you can, the feelings that accompanied these experiences. It may help if you keep an ongoing journal to record childhood memories. To help you remember, consider some of the following tools: dreams, music, nature, art, and visits to scenes from your childhood and adolescence.

5. Investigate further the connections between brain research and any of the 12 qualities of genius, such as creativity, curiosity, or imagination.

6. Devote part of each staff meeting to a study of 1 of the 12 dimensions of genius, or alternatively, create a 12-session study group with colleagues and devote a session each to discussing the 12 qualities.

P • A • R • T

2

THE GENIUS SHUTS DOWN

Many teachers will laugh at my premise that every student is a genius. In their experience, all too many students differ greatly from genius behavior, however one defines it. Teachers struggle daily with students who are antagonistic toward their efforts to teach them, who sleep through classes, who use their time to disrupt the class, and who appear to have no interest at all in learning. How could I ever, in my wildest imagination, say that these kids are geniuses? I do say this. But I say it with one important caveat: the genius is in hiding. If we could have seen many of these troubled and troublesome students when they were infants or young children, we would have very likely witnessed qualities of genius in them: joy, vitality, curiosity, creativity, and more. But something not so funny happened to them on their way to the classroom: their genius shut down.

To a greater or lesser extent the genius shuts down in just about everyone as they grow up. William Wordsworth described this process poetically when he wrote:

Our birth is but a sleep and a forgetting:

. . .

Heaven lies about us in our infancy!
Shades of the prison-house begin to close
    Upon the growing Boy
     But he
Beholds the light, and whence it flows,
    He sees it in his joy;
The Youth, who daily farther from the east
    Must travel, still is Nature's Priest,
    And by the vision splendid
    Is on his way attended;
At length the Man perceives it die away,
And fade into the light of common day.

—(FROM "ODE: INTIMATIONS OF IMMORTALITY").

We saw in the previous section how the rich web of neuronal connec-tions in the infant brain starts to diminish after age two. The child who "explodes" into language from two to five, learning thousands of words and an intricate language system, by adulthood is learning only about 50 words a year. Kids who excitedly enter school in kindergarten, full of the joy of learning, by senior high school all too often are stressed by competition, pressured by deadlines, and apathetic about anything related to the classroom. Pipher (1995) writes of preadolescent girls who are "interested in everything—sports, nature, people, music, and books." But according to Pipher, "Something dramatic happens to girls in early adolescence. Just as planes and ships disappear mysteriously into the Bermuda Triangle, so do the selves of girls go down in droves" (p. 19). In high school, students who shine academically are regarded as "geeks" or social outcasts, while appearing dumb is considered more socially cool (Natale 1995).

What happens to the genius of our kids? Why does it shut down?

This section will attempt to answer this question by looking at three institutions that bear a large part of the responsibility for this downward plunge: the home, the schools, and the popular media. Although these three institutions aren't the whole story (other culprits include influence of peers and related developmental factors), they are a large enough part to warrant extensive discussion; and although the home and popular media may seem to be largely outside of the influence of classroom teachers, one cannot hope to awaken the genius in students without having at least a basic understanding of their potent effects and a sense of how to deal with their presence in students' lives.

The Role of the Home

A student's home life represents his or her most powerful learning experience. If educators could expand their classrooms to the size of each student's neighborhood and hold classes 24 hours a day, they still would not have the impact on learning ability that a home does because of the all-important emotional bond between parent and child formed from the earliest moments of life. Researchers are now suggesting that important learning may begin *in utero* (Verny 1981, Chamberlain 1988, Noble 1993), and the first weeks and months of life are seen as crucial to a child's ability to learn. A substantial literature exists chronicling the importance of home influences on learning during the first three years of life (for a review, see Rutter 1985). One recent study even suggested that the number of words spoken to an infant by an engaged adult during the first year of life can have a tremendous impact upon later learning ability (Blakeslee, April 17, 1997). Studies of acknowledged adult geniuses and other highly competent individuals suggest that a stimulating early home life had a significant influence on later achievement (John-Steiner 1985, Bloom 1985). But while we've learned a great deal about the positive influences of the home, we've discovered even more about what can go wrong in the home to disrupt the genius qualities that are a child's natural birthright.

The following discussion of negative home influences focuses on four factors that are especially significant: (1) emotional dysfunction, (2) poverty, (3) a fast-paced lifestyle, and (4) rigid ideologies. Often, two or more of these factors combine in a family to make it even more difficult for a child or adolescent to express his or her genius, and they create disruptive patterns of thinking and behavior that kids inevitably bring to school with them.

Emotional Dysfunction

Some families have parents and other members who are crippled by emotional problems including alcoholism, drug dependence, food disorders, chronic rage, anxiety, and depression. The problems that these important role models carry tend to reverberate throughout the family system, setting up patterns of stress that come out as behavioral or learning problems in the children or adolescents who are members of it. Family systems proponents (see, for example, Bradshaw 1988, Satir 1988) view dysfunctional families as following certain basic rules that govern their attitude toward learning and growing; these include the need to be in control at all times; the need to be perfect; the need to blame others when things don't work out; and the denial of the ability to freely think, feel, perceive, choose, and imagine as one desires. Satir (1988) wrote that

> in troubled families, people's bodies and faces tell of their plight. Bodies are either stiff and tight, or slouchy. Faces look sullen, or sad, or blank like masks. Eyes look down and past people. Ears obviously don't hear. Voices are either harsh and strident or barely audible (p. 11).

In families with emotional dysfunction, a child's vitality is all too often crushed under a barrage of put-downs and insults, curiosity is punished or ignored, and joy is squashed under the heavy blanket of depression. Living in such conditions, children don't have the chance to explore, make mistakes, discover new ideas, and do the many other things that go along with being a genius. In families in which anxiety hovers over the home like a dark cloud, children lose their playfulness.

Alcohol- or drug-addicted parents create special problems that cripple the natural genius in children. Mothers who drink or use drugs during pregnancy damage the delicately evolving nervous system of the fetus, giving birth to children with fetal alcohol syndrome or drug-related brain damage. For example, Alessandri and his colleagues at the Medical College of Pennsylvania (November 1993) observed cocaine-exposed infants as having less joy during learning. Clearly in such cases kids are exposed to obstacles that limit their ability to express their intrinsic genius right from the moment they are born.

Poverty

Some families lack the material ability to provide stimulating learning environments for their children through no fault of their own but because of economic and social inequities. Maslow (1954) in his hierarchy of needs model suggests that one must first meet physiological and safety needs before moving on to higher needs such as self-esteem and self-actualization. Families in poverty must spend so much time during the day seeking adequate food, shelter, clothing, and other basics, that there is no energy available for nurturing the child's curiosity, creativity, or inventiveness. The very fact of the family's poverty often creates emotional stress that further depresses the joy and vitality of the child. Adult illiteracy in the family—caused by lack of access to adequate educational opportunities (see Kozol 1991, 1995)—makes it less likely that the children in the family will receive verbal and other forms of intellectual stimulation. In addition, problems such as poor prenatal care, malnutrition, and other factors commonly associated with poverty can damage the child's brain from the start of life, thereby limiting the potential to develop natural genius qualities.

Fast-Track Lifestyles

Many parents who have adequate financial resources and a solid educational background don't appear to have much time to spend with their kids because of their own hectic lives. Often very successful in their professions, these parents spend so much time trying to get ahead in their careers that they don't have any time left for their kids. When they do end up focusing on their children's learning life, they often think about how they can get their children on the fast track to success. Hence, families with a fast-paced lifestyle often pressure kids to learn things before they're ready for them. They start stimulating their kids right in the womb (see Van de Carr 1992), buy "teach your baby to read" books to use with their infants (see Doman 1964) and search for ways to speed up the learning process in older kids as well (see Ostrander and Schroeder 1979).

One of the consequences of this kind of pressure is that children develop stress symptoms, including anxiety, depression, headaches and stomachaches, nervous tics, and attention and learning difficulties. Elkind (1981) coined the term "hurried child syndrome" to describe the negative effects on children who are pushed to grow up too fast too soon, and he later extended his observations to adolescents (Elkind 1984). Because these kids aren't given time to naturally express their genius qualities in their own way, they can begin to retreat behind a facade of cynicism, apathy, or aggression. Many give up or burn out emotionally by the time they reach adolescence. Even though on the outside they may appear to be highly achieving students, their playfulness, curiosity, joy, and creativity have been all but destroyed.

Rigid Ideologies

Some families raise their children in an atmosphere of fear and hate toward those who do not share their own rigid belief systems. These belief systems may be on the right or the left politically; they may be related to any of the world's religions or be atheistic or philosophical in nature. What is at issue here is not the specific content of the belief system but the way children are taught to fear any other way of thinking and to hate those who stand outside of their own way of thinking. Allport (1954) studied the processes through which children develop prejudice and discovered it often emerges through the parent's use of powerful, emotionally loaded words that denigrate whole categories of people. In this kind of environment, children's natural curiosity about other ways of knowing and behaving is stopped in its tracks, their sensitivity to diversity is blunted, and their flexibility disappears. Prejudiced individuals, Allport observed, latch onto what is familiar, safe, simple, and definite. The genius of the child, which seeks to be inventive and creative, cannot flourish in such a family, and gives way to a closed and crippled attitude that, tragically, has already led to the deaths of hundreds of millions of people in the last century.

The intent in this description of negative family patterns is not to depress you but to raise your awareness as to how these home experiences function as actual teaching and learning events for the growing child and adolescent. Whether intended by the parent or not, the shaming of a child serves as a potent teaching tool, one that has in fact been used for thousands of years in many different cultures. A junk-strewn parking lot also functions as a learning environment, one that teaches danger, disorder, and (unwittingly) survival. Rather than simply lumping a student's myriad difficulties into the nonspecific category of "home problems," it's much more productive to regard the home environment as a learning environment—perhaps dangerous or barren or too fast-moving, but nevertheless the most powerful learning environment in that student's life. We need to understand that the reason why so many students seem to be anything but geniuses is because they have languished for so many years in home learning environments that have driven their genius underground.

The Role of the School

As suggested above, by the time many children enter school they have already had a good portion of their natural genius immobilized. However, the signs of genius still show themselves in kindergartners who thrill at the sight of a caterpillar during a science lesson, who fingerpaint with delight during art, and who raise their hands excitedly whenever the teacher asks a question. By the time those same students are seniors in high school, it's all too likely that they may be sitting stiffly and apathetically in their seats, unwilling to respond to a teacher's questions unless they are sure it will boost their grade point averages. New York University communication professor Neil Postman once wrote: "Children enter school as question marks and they leave school as periods." What happens in the interim? For many children who have had their genius suppressed during the first five years of home life, school may simply add insult to injury and even further repress their genius qualities. Four of the most significant school-related factors that help to shut down the genius in students are (1) testing and grading, (2) labeling and tracking, (3) textbook and worksheet learning, and (4) tedium.

Testing and Grading

Formal testing and grading systems have many important functions in education; however, developing the genius of students doesn't happen to be one of them. I believe that, of all the factors in education today, standardized testing is probably the single most inhibiting influence on the functioning of students' genius. Testing determines what students must learn, the rate at which they must learn, and the manner in which they must approach the content. Knowledge that may be exciting to the teacher and students, that ignites curiosity, wonder, creativity and joy, but that isn't included on the tests, is likely to be ignored or short-changed. One of the most frequent comments I hear from teachers in my workshops is, "I'd really like to do more of this exciting teaching and learning, but I can't take time for it—I have to get my kids ready for those high-stakes end-of-semester tests." Teachers sacrifice their own love of learning in an attempt to boost test scores for their school and thus keep administrators, school board members, parents, and politicians happy (or perhaps, more realistically, to keep them from becoming unhappy).

Standardized testing reduces the richness of a student's genius to numerical scores and percentiles. It creates stress in many students, and, as in the home environment, it is difficult to express the qualities of genius in an atmosphere of anxiety (how many students have reported feeling "joyful" during a test?). Testing is fundamentally a judgment on a student, and considerable research in the field of creativity suggests that this important genius quality does not flourish in an atmosphere of criticism, judgment, or evaluation; these factors, on the contrary, are some of the greatest cripplers of creativity (see, for example, Krippner 1967, Amabile 1979). Testing hardly ever provides room for a child to express imagination or inventiveness—in fact, the student is likely to be marked down for "little side trips of the mind" that show originality or ingenuity.

Grading systems are simply more chronic examples of testing—they come more frequently and in smaller doses, but this sometimes makes their effect even more devastating in helping to subdue a student's genius. Rather than regarding school assignments as opportunities to experience wonder, joy, or playfulness, students are taught to ask, "What do I need to do to get an A?" (Simon and Bellanca 1976, Yarborough and Johnson 1980, Hughes et al. 1985). Their curiosity becomes limited to finding out "what the teacher wants." Their sensitivity is blunted as they try to find out "what other people got" and "how I did compared to them" (Kirschenbaum et al. 1971). An entire attitude is created in the classroom that revolves around stratagems, maneuvers, tricks, and ploys that will earn the best grades (Holt 1970). Lost in all of this is the essential meaning of *genius:* such an atmosphere clearly does not give birth to the joy of learning.

Labeling and Tracking

The basic premise of this book is that every student is a genius. Labeling and tracking systems undermine this premise. They seek to sort kids into categorical programs and "ability groups," which while serving specific administrative needs do not generally benefit the students and certainly do not affirm their genius qualities unless they were lucky enough to be labeled "gifted" or placed into an "honors" program.

I have devoted considerable attention in my own writings to a critique of two of the most widely used educational labels in the United States: "learning disabilities" (Armstrong 1987b, 1988) and "attention deficit hyperactivity disorder" (Armstrong 1995, October 18, 1995, 1996a, 1996b). For the purposes of this book I am most concerned with the "dissing" qualities of these labels (*dis*abilities, *dis*order, *dys*function). These labels identify children and adolescents on the basis of what they *can't* do rather than what they *can* do. A child or adolescent may be highly creative, curious, inventive, sensitive, or playful and yet be identified by school officials as "disabled," even as research suggests that children labeled ADHD or LD do possess these kinds of positive attributes (see, for example, Tarver et al. 1980, Zentall 1988, West 1991, Cramond 1994). This labeling process creates attributional problems: the child, the child's peers, and the child's family all start to think about the child in terms of the negative label rather than in terms of any intrinsic genius quality. A substantial literature on the "self-fulfilling prophecy," "the halo effect," and "the placebo effect" (see, for example, Rosenthal and Rubin 1978) reveal how powerful one's beliefs can be in affecting self-concept, behavior, and even the academic performance of children in both regular and special education (Rosenthal and Jacobsen 1968, Foster et al. 1976, Coles 1987). Students who are already struggling with self-doubts have these problems compounded when their difficulties are institutionalized through formal labels.

Tracking is a more widespread and more subtle form of labeling. Instead of being labeled LD or ADHD, the student is placed in a program that may not even have a name, but, as students discern within a few minutes, that has a reputation for serving the needs of "slower" students with "less motivation," or students who are "at risk" for something or who need "extra help." The message is clear: You're not in this program because you are a genius; you're in it because you're not one. Research has shown that tracking systems are discriminatory, offer less challenging schoolwork, and are problematic in many other ways (Oakes 1985, Wheelock 1992). Such research suggests that "low-ability" classrooms provide fewer opportunities for higher-order thinking and place more emphasis on rote memorization and worksheet and workbook learning. Even "middle-ability" programs that cater to the "average" student treat students as "unspecial" and teach them in "unspecial" ways (Oakes and Lipton 1990, p. 163).

Textbooks and Worksheet Learning

It may be a great understatement to say that textbooks are not written by geniuses. They're written by committees. Often these committees have devoted considerable time and effort to avoiding controversy so as to placate different interest groups and thus ensure the books' adoption by the largest states in the union. As a result textbooks tend to be very bland, with little joy or vitality within their pages. Because they're written by committees, they have no personal voice that speaks directly to a student to inspire or stir a love of learning. Moreover, textbooks usually have to be returned at the end of the term, so students cannot write in them or form any kind of real emotional bond to their contents. Textbooks are unlikely to activate a student's curiosity, creativity, imagination, or wonder, and yet they structure 75 to 90 percent of all learning that goes on in our schools (Tyson-Bernstein 1988, Tyson and Woodward 1989). Most textbooks ought to be regarded as "genius-unfriendly" because they generally convey the message that knowledge is "information to be mastered," not mysteries to be plumbed or exciting terrain to explore.

Worksheets are even worse. Students spend their time filling in the blanks, circling the right item, drawing arrows from the apple to the A, and solving row after row of math problems instead of being curious, creative, or inventive with regard to the real world. Some children may go through an entire year of schooling filling out more than a thousand of these forms and bringing them home to parents who believe that worksheets represent meaningful learning experiences. Worksheets have nothing to do with genius. No genius ever attributed his or her success to a worksheet. No museum contains examples of great worksheets. These are bureaucratic devices that fit in well with an assembly-line model of education but do nothing to inspire, awaken, or enliven the genius of children or adolescents. No student has ever come back to a teacher after 30 years and said, "You were the teacher who changed my life! Ever since you showed me that worksheet with the A on one side and the apple on the other, my life has never been the same!" More likely, students' lives were changed for the worse when they came to school and discovered that the vitality of life had been reduced to an $8\frac{1}{2}$ **x** 11 inch piece of paper with specific commands printed on it. They find that their life has been changed for the worse by the message: There's no real work for geniuses in this place (see Smith 1986).

Tedium

If you were to pop your head into many classrooms around the United States and look for signs of the qualities of genius—joy, humor, vitality, creativity, playfulness—you might be sadly disappointed. All too many of our classrooms sacrifice these qualities in the name of instructional efficiency, classroom management, or meeting district timetables for educational outcomes. Goodlad in his monumental research project, *A Place Called School* (see Goodlad 1984), noted that the 1,000 classrooms visited were

> almost completely devoid of outward evidences of affect. Shared laughter, overt enthusiasm, or angry outbursts were rarely observed. Less than 3 percent of classroom time was devoted to praise, abrasive comments, expressions of joy or humor, or somewhat unbridled outbursts such as "wow" or "great" (pp. 229–230).

In such classrooms, many students turn off whatever genius qualities they still have and simply tune out. In one recent study (Csikszentmihalyi et al. 1993) researchers equipped high school students with beepers and told them they would be beeped randomly throughout the school day. When they heard the beep, the students were asked to stop and write down whatever was going on in their minds at the time (they were provided with special forms for this purpose). The researchers beeped

28 students who were engaged in a Chinese history lesson about Genghis Khan's invasion of China in the 12th century. Only two students were thinking about China: one was thinking about what he'd had at a Chinese restaurant two weeks before, and the other was wondering why Chinese men in the 12th century wore their hair in ponytails! Essentially, no one was thinking about the lesson or using their natural genius to engage with its content.

When tedium rules in a classroom, students divert their attention from the lesson plan and take their curiosity inside ("I wonder what Julie will be wearing to the dance this weekend?"). They activate their imagination to more interesting areas of their lives ("I'd love to be at the beach with the warm sun shining and blue sky and white sand . . .") and deploy their inventiveness in sneaky tricks like getting a friend's attention without being seen by the teacher. Their creativity may pop up in doodles in their notebooks, or little songs they're playing in their head, or romantic poems passed to a love interest. It takes a certain amount of genius to act as if one is involved in a lesson when one has absolutely no interest at all! The tragedy is that many teachers keep teaching as if nothing at all is wrong—as if apathy, boredom, pure procedure, and business-as-usual were the most natural ingredients in the world for a classroom rather than the major catastrophes they are for students' qualities of genius. The real message being communicated in the tedious classroom is that learning isn't joyful, education isn't alive, and wonder, wisdom, and humor have no place in the world of knowledge.

It isn't my intention to engage in an full-scale assault on an educational system that has already received far more criticism than it deserves. Much about our schools is very good indeed; many teachers are highly enthusiastic in sharing knowledge with their students; and many classrooms actively engage students in significant learning experiences that inspire joy, humor, wisdom, creativity, curiosity, and vitality. However, these things go on *in spite of* the above influences not *because of* them. It is certainly possible to defend testing, labeling, and textbooks as best practice in schools (e.g., labeling helps identify and serve students with special needs; testing provides valuable information about what students know and do not know about the curriculum; textbooks deliver information efficiently, etc.); but this is so only if the qualities of genius described in this book are regarded as having low value on an educator's list of priorities. If, on the other hand, the cultivation of every student's genius is considered of fundamental importance to learning, then we must regard the practices listed above with suspicion and develop ways of minimizing their negative impact on students' lives.

The Role of the Popular Media

If the negative influences of home and school represent a one-two combination punch to the genius of students, then the addition of popular media constitutes a veritable knockout blow. Over the past 40 years we've seen popular media change from an institution devoted to delivering knowledge about the world to a global force that has become a world in itself, increasingly dictating the nature of reality to its unwitting consumers.

Children and adolescents, being the most impressionable members of society, are those most at risk of being taken in by the powers of the media. And because most television programming, computer games, and Internet fare are not being created by geniuses to awaken curiosity, wonder, or wisdom, but are being fashioned by individuals more interested in making money and serving the lowest common denominator, our student's inborn genius is likely to find little nourishment from such influences. More likely, as Healy (1990) and others have increasingly pointed out, much popular media is actually endangering students' minds.

Educators must therefore educate themselves about those aspects of popular media that are most destructive to the qualities of genius described in this book, and seek to mediate those harmful influences as much as possible. Beyond the violent content of television and video games—which has received the greatest attention and has a huge research base demonstrating its harmful effects on children (see, for example, Singer and Singer 1981, Huesmann and Eron 1986, Comstock and Paik 1991)—at least three other more subtle but nevertheless devastating threats to the genius of students seem to emanate from the vast majority of TV, video, and Internet fare that kids are exposed to. These threats are (1) stereotypical images, (2) insipid language, and (3) mediocre content.

Stereotypical Images

The mass media heap out unrelenting doses of prefabricated images to children from the day they are first able to watch a TV or video screen until they graduate from high school or college. Most of these images have been developed by Hollywood, Silicon Valley, Madison Avenue, or other production centers where, for most of those involved, the idea of nurturing a child's or adolescent's inner genius has no meaning. There is little left for the imagination of the child or adolescent to do in the face of these ready-made logos, characters, plots, situations, and scenarios. As a result, kids simply sit back and passively drink in these images, which then proceed to seep into the subconscious only to emerge in school as stereotypical drawings, stories filled with clichés, and artificial and unreal conceptions of how the world works. Kids' inner imagination, one of those qualities of genius described above, eventually begins to atrophy through lack of use and eventually disappears entirely (see

Mander 1978; Singer and Singer 1981).

Popular media have also had a negative impact on another quality of genius: playfulness. One of the world's leading authorities on play, Brian Sutton-Smith (1986), wrote that the modern-day image of the child at play is of a single child watching a television set while playing with a battery-operated action toy. With so little for the child to actually *do* in this brave new world of automated playthings and preprogrammed entertainment, the genius of kids has fewer and fewer rich structures within which to develop into maturity.

Insipid Language

If one is looking for a good target to help explain the decline in students' ability to express themselves in writing or speaking, the popular media present themselves as an almost ideal candidate. The impact of this idea struck me recently while I was reading an article on Shakespeare in the *New York Review of Books* by Geoffrey O'Brien, executive director of the Library of America. O'Brien (1997) writes:

> Everyone who subscribes to cable television has had the experience of switching rapidly from channel to channel and hearing at every stop the same tones and inflections, the same vocabulary, the same messages: a language flattened and reduced to a shifting but never very large repertoire of catchphrases and slogans. . . . It is a dialect of dead ends and perpetual arbitrary switch-overs, intended always to sell but more fundamentally to fill time (p. 13).

O'Brien refers to this as the "homogenization of speech" and suggests that it lacks figurative language, rhetorical complexity, eloquence, word-play, or historical or literary allusion. Research cited earlier points to the strong role that early language experience from parents has on a child's learning ability; one must certainly include as part of this influence the language emanating from televisions and computers as well, because an infant may spend more time listening to these substitute parents than to the originals. And one must remember that parents' (and teachers') own language structures have been influenced by their years of contact with popular media. The end result of this homogenization of language is heard in students whose speech patterns are replete with phrases like "Yeah, right . . . " and "You know, then he went, like, you know . . . " and the ubiquitous, all-purpose response to society's complexities: "Whatever." Absent from these linguistic black holes is any attempt at playfulness, flexibility, imagery, humor, or other qualities that are the hallmark of real genius.

Mediocre Content

A frequently heard battle cry in education over the past few years has been the injunction that we must help our students cope with the "information explosion" that has occurred with the rise of new technologies including the Internet and satellite television. This is certainly true, and the first and most important thing we should teach students is how much junk there is to avoid. Fifty years ago, Newton Minnow, chairman of the Federal Communications Commission, characterized television programming as a giant "wasteland." This image, reminiscent of T. S. Eliot, can now be extended to include much of what is found in video and computer games and on the Internet (Healy 1990, Murray 1997).

The cumulative force of such mediocrity has created a commonly shared culture based on the trivial and the base. In my own workshops for educators I sometimes ask participants to raise their hands if they recognize any of the following names: Wole Soyinka, Naguib Mahfouz, Kenzaburo Oe, and Wislawa Szymborska. Generally few people raise their hands. Then I ask them to raise their hands if they recognize this set of names: O. J. Simpson, Timothy McVeigh, Tonya Harding, and

Joey Buttafuoco. Most people raise their hands. I then point out that the first set of names represent recent winners of the Nobel Prize in literature, and the second set of names are those of people who have been accused or convicted of civil or criminal offenses in the United States. (As time goes by, the recognition of some of these latter names may fade, only to be replaced by a new set of uncivil celebrities.)

What do we value in our society? What do we pay most attention to? Clearly, the popular media have already made the decision for many of us and our students. It repeatedly focuses the attention of its viewers and listeners on mediocre topics (e.g., movie stars breaking up), negative values (e.g., glorification of violence), and less than admirable role models (see above). Children and adolescents thrive in this media-fed popular culture that extols not the most creative, the most joyful, or the most wise individuals (those who manifest genius in its many forms), but those who are often the sleaziest, the rottenest, and the most devious among us. This causes our students' inner genius (which craves the inspiration of positive role models and uplifting themes and ideas) to go into hiding.

Some people will argue that my indictment of popular media is unjust because there are plenty of examples of excellent television programming (e.g., *Masterpiece Theater*), high-quality computer games (e.g., "Voyage of the Mimi"), and excellent Internet sites. This is very true, and it is incumbent upon educators to know where these resources are located and to help students find them and gain maximum benefit from them. However, against the backdrop of the totality of mass media and popular culture, these examples of excellence are like a few grains of sand thrown against the winds of the Sahara. Moreover, although superb programming exists and is growing every day, staring at a screen or clicking a keyboard, mouse, or joystick still pales in comparison with the more tried-and-true building blocks of genius: contact with inspiring people and exposure to compelling situations, stimulating materials, and challenging problem-solving opportunities that arise out of daily life (see Brod 1984, Davy 1984, Cuffaro 1984). It is to these elements and the cultivation of each student's genius that we now turn in the final section of this book.

For Further Study

1. Think of a student that you have worked with who has shown one or more of the qualities of genius listed in this book (e.g., creativity, vitality, joy, humor, curiosity, etc.) but who now seems to have shut down these qualities. Is it possible to pinpoint when this happened? Did it happen gradually or are there specific events associated with the loss? Spend some time writing about this student's loss of genius and then share your thoughts with a colleague.

2. Recollect times in your own life when you felt that certain qualities of genius in yourself were stymied, paralyzed, criticized, or in other ways undermined. What were the results of these negative experiences (e.g., did you shut down that quality? hide it? modify it so that it became more acceptable to others? develop it to an even greater extent?). Write down these experiences and your reaction to them. If you wish, share these with a trusted colleague.

3. Discuss the negative influences of home life on the genius of the students that you work with in your educational setting. Without blaming the families involved, explore how factors like emotional dysfunction and poverty make it difficult for some of your students to develop to their fullest potential as geniuses.

4. Explore the impact that standardized testing has on your students' willingness to be creative, curious, inventive, imaginative, or to display in other ways the qualities of genius discussed in this book. What role

does standardized testing have on your own ability to provide experiences and resources that expand the genius of your students?

5. Examine the policy in your school of labeling students as "learning disabled," "ADHD," or other related terms, or of tracking students into so-called lower-ability groups. What impact has labeling or tracking had on the ability of individual students in these programs to express their qualities of genius? What has been done in your school to help put the focus on the positive genius qualities of children in special education or in the so-called lower tracks?

6. Discuss the effects of the popular mass media (television, video games, the Internet), on your students' lives both inside and outside of the classroom. What impact of the popular media have you seen in the drawings, writings, or speech patterns of your students? What influence do you think the popular media has had on the expression of the qualities of genius in your students?

3

HOW TO AWAKEN GENIUS IN THE CLASSROOM

I realize that many of you reading this book up to this point may be feeling somewhat downhearted by the many roadblocks described in the previous section. I'd like to remind you, however, that even in the most troubled and troublesome of learners the genius is still alive—somewhere. It may be buried under loads of put-downs, negative evaluations, low grades and test scores, delinquent behavior, self-hatred, and more, but like the seed in winter that lies dormant while braving the toughest storms and coldest arctic spells only to blossom with the sun's warmth in the spring, this genius too can survive if you will take the time to study the optimum conditions for its growth in the classroom.

Some educators may argue that not much can be accomplished in many students after so much damage has been done in the home during the first few years of life or as a result of the negative influence of popular media and culture. These protests, although convincing to some, often mask an unwillingness to even *begin* the work that must occur in order for educators to help reawaken the genius of their students.

There are actually only a few simple principles to guide you in your efforts. These principles represent ideas that have been around for a long time—part of the common wisdom that good teachers have always drawn upon for inspiration in carrying out the important work of educating young minds. Although they may be phrased differently in other contexts or divided into a greater or lesser number, I've found these four principles to be especially useful in thinking about how to awaken genius in the classroom:

- Reawaken the genius in yourself.
- Provide simple genius experiences in the classroom.
- Create a genial climate in the classroom.
- Know that genius is expressed in many ways.

Reawaken the Genius in Yourself

The most powerful way to awaken genius in the classroom has nothing at all to do with lesson plans, classroom environment, learning materials, or instructional time. It has to do with you. And not you as an educator, but you as a human being. If you wish to spark the hidden light of genius that lives in every one of your students, you must first find and (re)light that spark in yourself. More than 40 years ago, Arthur Jersild wrote a book entitled *When Teachers Face Themselves* (1955). This remarkable work argued that until teachers look within themselves and learn to deal with their own inner lives (their joys and sorrows, hopes and anxieties, etc.), their task of teaching will be very difficult. Even further back, in the 1920s, German educator Rudolf Steiner (1982) said very much the same thing: "What kind of school plan you make is neither here nor there; what matters is what sort of person you are" (p. 32).

Above all, educators need to look at the qualities of genius in their own lives—vitality, joy, humor, creativity, wonder, and more—and ask which of these are burning bright and which have been dimmed by years of neglect. Much has been made in the press of arteriosclerosis, or hardening of the arteries. A much more serious condition exists in our culture that Montagu (1983) calls *psychosclerosis*, or hardening of the mind. How many educators who enjoin their students to be good readers haven't themselves enjoyed reading a book for pleasure in years? How many teachers ask students to be high achievers in math and science but themselves lack any enthusiasm for the great discoveries being made in those fields or no longer ask the basic wide-eyed questions about the universe or about the origins of life that have inspired the greatest scientists of every age? My own sad experience as a novice teacher entering a teacher's lounge was to discover veteran teachers discussing not Freud, Plato, Mozart, or the theory of relativity but teacher retirement plans, collective bargaining disputes, and the latest gossip about students and fellow teachers! These were the senior members of the school, and what were they modeling for the new recruits? Stagnation, not inspiration! Since then, I've read of all too many cases of teachers who were spurned by their colleagues for showing too much creativity, outspokenness, innovation, and vitality (see, for example, Bradley 1995).

Another ailment, related to psychosclerosis, is *cainotophobia*—the fear of new things. How easy it is for teachers to settle into a routine of instruction, collect a paycheck every week, and stop thinking, growing, and learning about how the world works. Yet this is precisely what our students need from us more than anything else—to be curious, awake, and alive to the world!

This kind of enthusiasm is contagious—students catch it from teachers who have it. It's your own genius nature that students will carry away with them and remember you for 30 years from now. It's not likely they'll remember you for the specific content of the curriculum (e.g., "You were the one who taught me to conjugate Latin verbs!"). What will likely have the greatest impact on your students will be your own vitality and creativity ("You helped us create plays about literature—that experience never left me!"), as well as your ability to acknowledge and develop their natural genius qualities ("You were the one who helped me to believe in myself!"). This inspirational quality has been chronicled well in many of the greatest movies about teaching ever made, in characters such as Mr. Chips (*Goodbye, Mr. Chips*), Jean Brodie (*The Prime of Miss Jean Brodie*), Jamie Escalante (*Stand and Deliver*), John Keating (*Dead Poets Society*), and Mark Thackeray (*To Sir with Love*). These teachers offered something different—a measure of uniqueness and even an offbeat quality—that helped them make a significant impact on their students' lives.

So, how do you recapture that spark and sizzle if it has indeed disappeared from your life? Like your students, you have probably had your genius shut down by the same kinds of home, school, and cultural influences described earlier, and you need to devote some time to finding it again. Simply being aware of what fills your life with the greatest interest and passion can help to launch this search. What kinds of experiences put you into a "flow state"? Reading books? Painting? Hiking? Listening to music? Sometimes it can be helpful to remember your dreams for clues about what fills you with energy and excitement, or to remember your own childhood and adolescence, when you might have been passionately involved in hobbies, arts, or other activities that you've neglected over the years.

The life of the Swiss psychoanalyst Carl Jung provides a good example of how reminiscence can powerfully ignite creativity. In his late 30s, Jung went through a severe depression as a result of ending his relationship with his mentor, Sigmund Freud. One day, he had a dream that reminded him of how he used to play as a child creating miniature worlds out of water, sand, and rocks at the lakeside beaches near his boyhood home. His response to the dream was to actually devote some time each day after work to playing in a very similar way: he began to create little cities with stones on the banks of Lake Zurich next to his home. He discovered that this process of playing filled him with new ideas that fueled his creative work over the next 40 years (Jung 1963).

Once you've hit upon at least one or two revitalizing activities that you'd like to bring into your life, start immediately to put these experiences into action. As the German poet Goethe once wrote: "Whatever you can do, or dream you can, begin it. Boldness has genius, power, and magic in it." Here is a very partial list of activities that might start you on this journey to the center of your own genius:

- reading for pleasure
- keeping a journal
- writing poetry or stories
- listening to music
- taking up a musical instrument
- learning to paint or draw
- joining a choir
- traveling
- building furniture
- designing and sewing clothes
- attending concerts or lectures
- taking courses at a local college
- listening to books on tape
- learning how to meditate
- learning calculus through computer software
- joining a book club

- doing volunteer work at a community center
- engaging in nature study
- building electronics from kits
- running for office in your community
- learning a competitive sport such as tennis or golf
- watching classic movies
- studying a particular historical period
- taking up photography
- solving mathematical puzzles or brainteasers
- following current developments in science
- starting or joining an investment club
- studying art, history, or literature
- backpacking in the wilderness
- learning a new language
- watching how-to videos to learn a new skill
- starting a classical music collection
- joining a theatrical production
- going into psychotherapy
- joining an interest group on the Internet
- cultivating your spiritual life
- planning a garden
- studying philosophy
- starting a business
- joining Toastmasters or another speaking group
- starting a collection (e.g., stamps, old posters)
- learning how to fix things around the house
- inventing something and then patenting it
- taking dance classes
- writing a column for a newsletter or newspaper
- creating a special-interest club

- taking up stargazing
- attending a retreat
- creating a video in an area of interest
- learning a new style of cooking

To help get you started with some of these activities, here's a list of some of my favorite resources for lighting the genius fires in specific areas of interest:

- Betty Edwards, *Drawing on the Right Side of the Brain: A Course in Enhancing Creativity and Artistic Confidence*. New York: Tarcher/Putnam, 1979. This popular book shows how to dramatically improve drawing ability even among those who feel they can't draw at all.
- Outward Bound, Route 9D, R2 Box 280, Garrison, NY 10524-9757; 1-800-243-8520. This organization provides programs all over the United States in a variety of outdoor activities including sailing, mountaineering, kayaking, and whitewater rafting.
- Books on Tape, P.O. Box 7900, Newport Beach, CA 92658; 1-800-626-3333. This company provides the largest selection of unabridged audio books available. If you don't have time to read at home, listen to these cassettes on your way to work in your car. You can listen to the entire *Brothers Karamazov* by Fyodor Dostoevsky on 29 hour-and-a-half cassettes!
- *The Guide to Writers Conferences*. ShawGuides Inc., 625 Biltmore Way, Suite 1406, Coral Gables, FL 33134; 305-446-8888 or 1-800-247-6553. For the teacher who is writing a novel, poetry, or plays, or is just starting to explore his or her own writing voice, this book includes comprehensive listings of writers conferences, workshops, seminars, residencies, retreats, and writers organizations.
- The Teaching Company, 7405 Alban Station Court, Suite A107, Springfield, VA 22150-2318; 1-800-832-2412. This organization sells

and rents more than 60 audio and video courses by some of the best university professors in the country in areas such as philosophy, fine arts, science, religion, math, literature, and history. Includes such titles as "How to Understand and Listen to Great Music" and "The Great Minds of the Western Intellectual Tradition."

• Movies Unlimited, 6736 Castor Avenue, Philadelphia, PA 19149-2184; 1-800-4-MOVIES; fax: 215-725-3683. This is the source for the most comprehensive mail-order catalog of movies available, including most of the great classic and foreign films of all time, as well as films in the performing arts, documentaries, how-to videos, and concert videos.

• Howard Rheingold, *The Millennium Whole Earth Catalog Access to Tools and Ideas for the Twenty-First Century*. San Francisco: Harper, 1994. This book presents a rich collection of resources (books, organizations, videos, kits, and other materials) in a wide range of fields, including ecology, science, learning, psychology, multiculturalism, and arts and crafts.

• Ron Gross, *The Independent Scholar's Handbook*. Berkeley, Calif.: Ten Speed Press, 1993. This wonderful book shows readers how to take an area of interest and become a leading expert in it. It's the best book on adult self-motivated learning that I've ever seen.

• Clifton Fadiman and John S. Major, *The New Lifetime Reading Plan*. 4th ed. New York: HarperCollins, 1997. This book lists more than 100 authors, from Homer and Shakespeare to Joyce and Woolf, that one could profitably spend much of one's life studying.

These resources and suggested activities are only a start to help direct you toward developing your own genius. The point is not to saddle yourself with a new list of things you have to do, read, or write for, but rather to allow yourself to be directed toward those activities that you want to do for their own sake. The noted American mythologist Joseph Campbell enjoined people to "follow your bliss . . . then doors will open up where you didn't know there were doors." This is what it means to awaken the genius in yourself—to discover those experiences in life that make you feel more alive and that give you a sense of greater richness and meaning in the world.

As you fill up with new life, your students will notice the difference and be profoundly affected by it. I remember as an elementary school student how vibrant my music teacher Miss Wilds appeared after a trip to Hawaii and how the excitement of her sharing that experience with us remains with me to this very day. This gift of your own vitality is the greatest thing you can give your students to remind them that they too possess this precious jewel of genius.

Provide Simple Genius Experiences

It may seem implausible to some educators that the most effective way to draw out the genius in students is by using *simple* experiences rather than complex and sophisticated techniques. As educators, we are accustomed to expecting that highly positive learning outcomes must be associated with detailed programs, intensive preparations, and intricate plans. However, a look at the life histories of many of the acknowledged geniuses of the world reveals that it was *simple* materials and experiences that inspired them to follow their life's work. For Albert Einstein, it was when his father showed him a simple magnetic compass when he was five years old. Einstein wrote later that this experience filled him with wonder and started him off on his quest to discover the mysteries of the universe (Clark 1984). For Yehudi Menuhin, it was when his parents took him to see a concert of the San Francisco Symphony Orchestra when he was almost four. He later wrote that he was enthralled with the performance and asked his parents to give him a violin for his birthday and to make the man who played the violin on stage his own teacher (Walters and Gardner 1986). For Frank Lloyd Wright it was playing with wooden blocks as a child (Provenzo and Brett 1983). For Martha Graham, it was a performance by Ruth St. Denis in Santa Barbara, California, when Graham was 14 that awakened her to her destiny as a dancer (Gardner 1993b). For the Russian painter Wassily Kandinsky, it was a box of oil colors purchased for pennies as a child (Werner 1948).

I could go on to detail many more of these types of experiences (they represent a powerful range of learning situations that educational researchers would do well to further explore). The point is that these sources of inspiration were not kits or sophisticated learning programs or projects. They were simple resources and events from real life. I am suggesting that these kinds of materials and experiences are often the most powerful ones in awakening genius not just in the "official geniuses" of society but in everyone, including your students. That doesn't mean we need some manufacturer to create a special "genius box" for the classroom filled with a magnetic compass, some wooden blocks, and tickets for the symphony! The materials and experiences you choose for your classroom should be appropriate for your students' age group and should reflect your own natural interests and passions as well as those of your students (and yet, too, many captivating materials derive their power from taking the class totally by surprise). The following list may help you get started in thinking about the kinds of resources you can provide (see also the Selected Resources at the end of the book):

- recordings of significant music
- reproductions of great art
- historical relics
- simple math puzzles (e.g., a Möbius strip)
- fauna and flora
- classic movies
- performances of great theater or dance
- prize-winning documentaries

- readings from great literature
- recordings of the work of eminent poets
- simple machines
- artifacts from other cultures
- art materials
- building supplies
- simple science tools (e.g., a magnet, a lens)
- a Polaroid camera
- storytelling
- miniaturized models (e.g., of cities, inventions)
- a fascinating visitor
- magic tricks
- personal memorabilia or recollections (e.g., old photos)
- an unusual question or puzzle
- materials to smell, taste, or touch
- conversations with the class on significant topics
- unusual things to listen to or see (e.g., illusions)
- a tape recorder (e.g., to record voices and play back)
- an absorbing project
- an imaginary journey
- experiences in nature
- field trips to museums or concerts
- a classroom theater production
- special books
- visits with exceptional individuals (e.g., an artist)
- simple musical instruments
- significant in-class friendships

Most of these resources can be adapted for use at any grade or age level and for any content area by a teacher who sees the possibilities inherent in them (see, for example, Armstrong 1994, for classroom activities based upon multiple intelligences theory). Their importance, though, lies not in making the materials immediately relevant to the existing curriculum (this can serve to restrict your choices). Rather, it lies in evoking in students qualities of genius such as wonder, humor, joy, creativity, and vitality.

Find materials that have the ability to surprise your students, to wake them up to a new perspective, to shock them into a different way of perceiving or thinking, to delight them with a fresh point of view, or to excite them with a strong surge of feelings or ideas. Bringing an unusual pet into a class of 3rd graders is guaranteed to create a wave of excitement! Showing a group of 12th graders a dissected human brain (brought in by a professional researcher) is bound to create a ripple of interest! Yet one mustn't try to reach only for shock value (an all-too-common impulse fed by the popular media). Many of the genius experiences you provide for your students may appear to have no impact; but in a small group of students or even in one individual, they may quietly incubate for many years before having a profound influence.

If you wish, you can have a regular time during the day for "genius experiences" (a teacher version of show-and-tell). However, it may be more appropriate to let these experiences simply weave in and out of the classroom day without announcement or fanfare. The more of these kinds of simple experiences you provide in the classroom over a period of time, the greater the chances that some of them will take root and work their miracles within your students' minds.

Create a Genial Climate in the Classroom

Far more important to the awakening of genius than specific resources and experiences are the broader attitudes and overall atmosphere of the classroom. I've chosen to describe this desired ambiance as "genial" because of its association with the word *genius*. The *Compact Oxford*

English Dictionary (1991) gives several interrelated meanings for *genial*, including "festive," "conducive to growth," "enlivening," "jovial," and "pertaining to 'genius' or natural disposition." Each of these meanings captures an aspect of the mood that I believe every classroom should foster to help students realize their full potential as geniuses.

A person walking into a genial classroom knows almost at once that it is a place dedicated to the celebration of learning and young minds; a cognitive greenhouse, so to speak, that honors and celebrates the capacities of each and every student. In a genial classroom, there are frequent outbursts of energy representing students' exuberance in discovering something new, in making novel connections, in confronting and overcoming challenges, in being surprised or delighted, intrigued or mystified, and indignant or outspoken about the ideas and materials being presented. This contrasts sharply with the non-genial classroom in which strictness, rigidity, boredom, criticism, or anxiety stifles the creative impulse and strangles any possibility for joy, humor, flexibility, or vitality.

I believe that all genial classrooms share at least five characteristics that guide their instruction regardless of content or grade level. These characteristics are (1) freedom to choose, (2) open-ended exploration, (3) freedom from judgment, (4) honoring of every student's experience, and (5) belief in every student's genius.

Freedom to Choose

It's hard to imagine external authorities telling any of the great geniuses of our culture—Einstein, Beethoven, or Goethe, for example—how to think and study in order to do their best work. Einstein, in fact, felt greatly relieved when he escaped the authoritarian Prussian school system as a teenager and discovered a school in Switzerland that allowed him greater latitude of thought (Clark 1984). Yet, all too often, we give our own budding geniuses too little room to choose the conditions of their own best learning. We tell them what they are to study, how they are to study it, and what will happen to them if they don't study it. I'm reminded of a colleague's remark at a recent conference: "Schools, prisons, and mental hospitals are the only institutions in society where if you don't go, they come to get you." Students who aren't given significant choices about what they can learn or how they are able to learn it soon either give in and adapt, or give up and tune out. In both cases, the qualities of genius have virtually no room for expression. An 11th grade student who gets to choose whether to do a final project in history as a paper, a play, a photographic essay, or a hands-on demonstration has the opportunity to display creativity in a way that simply isn't possible when every student is required to turn in a 15-page essay. A 2nd grader who looks forward to a 30-minute "choice time" every day to pick from a variety of activity centers involving drawing, building, relating, writing, singing, and dramatizing has far more opportunity to experience curiosity than one who follows a lock-step sequence of courses throughout the day.

In the genial classroom, freedom to choose does not mean that students are left to fend for themselves. Choices are carefully designed within safe and clear structures so that kids can experience the delight of having a limited number of choices to make instead of needing to decide every moment what to do (shades of the free-school movement of the 1960s!). The important point is that students feel *empowered* when they make choices, and this inner power is the genius rousing itself up from its long slumber, ready to meet the world head on (see Adelman et al. 1990, Rejskind 1982).

Open-Ended Exploration

Just as students should be able to make significant choices in their learning, they also need to be allowed to explore a subject without necessarily having to reach a fixed end point. This runs counter to established practice in many classrooms around the country where teachers have been trained to ask questions to elicit certain definite responses, to give tests that have precise answers, and to develop instructional strategies containing fixed outcomes. The overarching instructional metaphor that rules all too many classrooms is of an arrow moving horizontally across space from the left to the right (or perhaps ascending like a corporate graph depicting rising profits). Real learning—the learning of geniuses—is not at all like that. It's characterized by multiple arrows moving in many different directions. To study the progress of the work of the acknowledged geniuses of our culture reveals, in fact, many dead-ends, stagnations, resignations, cross-outs, and regressions, along with the bursts of insight and the incremental progressions that moved them along (Gardner 1993b).

The genial classroom recognizes this kind of uncharted learning curve and even encourages it through open-ended questions, simple experiences and materials (like those listed earlier) that can give rise to a number of possible explorations, and class projects that may evolve over time into endeavors far different than those originally envisioned (for example, a 3rd grade project on interviewing grandparents that turns into a history of the community). This open-ended attitude toward learning encourages flexibility in thinking (one of the qualities of genius) and prepares students for the real world (where fixed outcomes are a rare commodity) far better than the safer, more predictable lessons and objectives of the non-genial classroom.

Freedom from Judgment

The genial classroom allows students to learn in an atmosphere free of criticism and judgment. In fact, research demonstrates that creativity cannot fully flourish in an atmosphere in which students feel they are being evaluated, judged, or tested (Krippner 1967, Amabile 1979, Kohn 1993). Consequently, the genial classroom avoids as much as possible the use of grades and standardized testing based on "norms" to which every student must be compared. This sort of ranking system ignores the intrinsic genius of every student, seeking rather to lift some students up to elite status and to demote others to an inferior position.

In cases in which testing and grades are required because of political or administrative needs, genial classroom teachers may assist students in learning how to succeed within that framework, but they always remember that their true mission is to focus on the intrinsic joy of learning and to continually remind their students that what is truly important in life is not high grades or test scores but an awakened mind and a vital attitude toward learning. Genial classroom teachers may even provide frequent times during the day or week that are "test-free" or "grade-free," when students may engage in learning activities without having to worry about the impact of their explorations on their grade point average or end-of-semester test results.

Honoring Every Student's Experience

In a genial classroom, students' ideas, explorations, and creative efforts are honored regardless of whether they fit in with the experiences of the teacher, the other students, or the wider social community. I'm reminded of how Jean Piaget's early work with Alfred Binet in Paris led to his fascination with the *wrong* answers that students gave on Binet's I.Q. tests. Instead of disregarding these responses, Piaget sought to enter into the world of each student to discover the nature of his or her inner thinking processes—an investigative style that ultimately led to his important developmental theories.

This is the sort of attitude that a genial classroom takes toward the growing mind of each student. Students' ideas are respected, listened to, and celebrated. A 1st grade student who says that the sun is hot because there is a man inside of it who makes fire isn't dismissed out of hand and told the "correct" scientific answer; instead her teacher may tell her some multicultural stories that are very close to her own response, and lead her to wonder about her ideas with further open-ended questions and activities (e.g., "Does a stove or a campfire have a man inside of it?"). A 10th grader who argues in class that UFOs exist isn't hooted down or ridiculed by the class but rather is allowed to present his evidence in a project format and to argue his case before his peers. Even prejudices, stereotypes, and other beliefs that may not be politically correct in today's social climate receive an opportunity to be aired in a genial classroom, so that their fullest implications may be explored in an atmosphere of trust, mutual understanding, and diversity of opinion.

By respecting each student's experience, the genial classroom teacher gains access to the inner thoughts, fantasies, images, and feelings of students. The teacher gives permission to students to bring those contents as fully into the classroom as possible, where they can be expressed and interacted with, and where they can ultimately transform and be transformed by the other genius minds in the classroom.

Believing in Every Student's Genius

In the genial classroom, the teacher holds an *unqualified* belief in the genius of every student. She doesn't take the attitude: "All students are geniuses, but some students are more geniuslike than others." She presides over a democracy of geniuses, so to speak, where every student is equal in their geniushood, while at the same time each student expresses his or her genius in a very different way. She also avoids the pitfall of officially declaring that "every student is a genius" while privately bewailing their shortcomings or in actual classroom practice treating them as less than brilliant.

The genial classroom teacher practices what she preaches. Like Michelangelo, who saw the angel in the bare rock before he started sculpting, the genial teacher sees the seeds of genius residing in each student regardless of labels, psych reports, complaints from other teachers, test results, or overt signs of less than genius behavior in class. She practices Goethe's dictum that if you "treat people as if they are what they ought to be, you help them to become what they are capable of being." She serves as an advocate for each student among the unbelievers in the student's life, which may include parents, other teachers, peers, or administrators. Most importantly, she serves as a coach to each student to remind them of who they really are, to speak words similar to those of Pablo Casals, who once remarked:

> What do we teach students in school? We teach them that two and two make four and that Paris is the capital of France. When will we also teach them what they are? We should say to each of them: Do you know what you are? You are a marvel! . . . In the millions of years that have passed, there has never been another person like you. You could become a Shakespeare, a Michelangelo, a Beethoven. You have the capacity for anything. Yes, you are a marvel (Casals April 1983, p. 101).

This message given in a genuine spirit to each student could effect a transformation in learning far greater than any current educational reform.

Know That Genius Is Expressed in Many Ways

For many teachers, perhaps the greatest difficulty in seeing each of their students as geniuses lies in the limited definition of genius that they may retain even after reading this book. The traditional notion of genius as representing an elite few still has a strong hold upon our consciousness, and, perhaps more ominously, still lurks in the shadows of our unconscious, where it is much more difficult to eradicate. That's why it's crucial for each teacher to expand his or her ideas of genius and giftedness beyond the traditional notion of I.Q.

This book has attempted to transform the term *genius* by moving it closer to its root etymological meanings (e.g., "to give birth to") and by expanding its sense to include at least 12 different qualities that are part of everyone's birthright. However, I don't believe that this is enough to convince teachers of the real genius of every student. To effect a real transformation in thinking, teachers need to see more concrete examples of what the genius in students looks like. I.Q. testing has always had appeal because it put in bold numbers the potential of each student. We need to develop something equally bold (but non-numerical) in characterizing the genius of each of our students. Consequently, I suggest that we turn to a wide range of learning models to give us the broadest possible language with which to speak about the varieties of giftedness or genius in our students.

Over the past 30 years, many learning models have succeeded in describing different kinds of giftedness other than the traditional I.Q. variety of brilliance (see Taylor 1968, Guilford 1977, Dunn and Dunn 1978, Carini 1982, Gardner 1983, Sternberg 1988, Bloom 1985, Renzulli 1986, McCarthy 1987). I personally feel that the theory of multiple intelligences comes closest to providing educators with a model that embraces a wide range of gifts in our students that are also represented in actual roles in the real world. In its current form, the theory of multiple intelligences posits the existence of eight basic intelligences: linguistic, logical-mathematical, spatial, bodily-kinesthetic, musical, interpersonal, intrapersonal, and naturalist (Gardner 1983, 1996). Each of these intelligences can serve as a context for describing a variety of gifts in students. The following 63 roles represent a partial list of possible forms of "genius" in the classroom in the broad sense used in this book:

• *Linguistic Intelligence:* the bookworm, the poet, the storyteller, the orator, the humorist, the test taker, the trivia expert, the super-speller, the playwright, the raconteur

• *Logical-Mathematical Intelligence:* the computer programmer, the super-calculator, the math whiz, the scientist, the logician, the rationalist, the chess player

• *Spatial Intelligence:* the inventor, the artist, the cartoonist, the photographer, the mechanical wizard, the designer, the visualizer or daydreamer, the map maker

• *Bodily-Kinesthetic Intelligence:* the athlete, the dancer, the actor, the craftsperson, the mime, the sculptor, the human pretzel, the sportsperson, the hands-on learner

• *Musical Intelligence:* the singer, the songwriter, the guitarist (or player of any instrument), the rapper, the rhythm ace, the musical library (of songs), the acute listener

• *Interpersonal Intelligence:* the natural leader, the class mediator, the negotiator, the manipulator, the social director, the human barometer (of affective feelings in another person), the sympathetic friend, the highly moral or political student

• *Intrapersonal Intelligence:* the entrepreneur, the freelancer, the different drummer, the independent spirit, the visionary, the goal setter, the reflective thinker, the futurist

• *Naturalist Intelligence:* the lizard expert (or expert on any specific fauna or flora), the nature enthusiast, the pet lover, the collector, the hunter, the scout

Even this list is quite limited. We might add to it all of the thousands of possible career and positive lifestyle roles found in adults around the world and envision student versions of them in the classroom as precursors (for example, the genius of the electrical engineer manifested in the student who is particularly apt at creating inventions using electricity, or the abilities of the herbal healer prefigured in the student who has a knowledge of plants). Further, when we enter the arena of the personal intelligences or "emotional intelligence" (Goleman 1995), an even greater array of subtly nuanced traits and characteristics represents a whole new treasure box of gifts. As educator Hugh Mearns once put it: "Each one of us has a gift. There is . . . the tortoise gift of the plodder, the fox gift of cunning, the dog gift of faithfulness, the song-sparrow gift of cheerfulness, the swan gift of beauty in motion" (Mearns 1958). Some students have a gift for appreciating great beauty, others for dealing with disappointment or showing special courage or persistence. Some students even have a special genius for making trouble in the classroom!

When looking for broader definitions of giftedness such as those described above, it's especially important to avoid the trap of overcategorizing—regardless of how diverse the categories might be. I've become concerned about educators using the theory of multiple intelligences to label students as "linguistic" or as "the spatial group" or "the BK [Bodily-Kinesthetic] learners." These labels, though positive, still limit our understanding of each student's true genius. Even more specific labels like "the bookworm," "the dancer," or "the smiler" allow in only a small portion of the total student and block out much else that might be worthy.

The truth is that each student has the potential to demonstrate many forms of genius in the classroom (assuming the existence of a genial climate that allows them to do so). Ultimately, then, the most fine-grained analysis of a student's genius would consist of a description of that student's particular uniqueness in the world—a pattern of uniqueness that, as Casals put it, has never existed before in the universe and never will exist again. This means that there are as many forms of genius in the classroom as there are students.

I close this short volume with a renewed emphasis on the power that this kind of thinking can have on transforming our classrooms and our world. We have given much attention in the past two decades to the destruction of rain forests around the globe. These precious ecosystems are said to contain plants that hold cures to disease and pestilence, and the bulldozers of greed are wiping out these possibilities acre by acre with every passing day. The field of learning has its own endangered ecosystem represented by our students' *brain forests*. There are so many students who have wonderful gifts to share but who may never be recognized by anyone. Right now in your classroom you may have a student who has the potential to someday develop a vaccine for AIDS, or to create a plan to combat world starvation, or to develop a project aimed at quelling a nuclear holocaust. This student may not currently be seen as one of the gifted ones in your classroom. In fact, he or she may actually be one of those kids with a "disability" label or a reputation for laziness. If you embrace the notion that genius is just for the elite few, you might let this student slip by unrecognized, and that gift might be lost to the world. On the other hand, if you regard each one of your students as a true genius—each in his or her own way—and create a classroom environment where that genius can be identified, nurtured, and made available to others, there's no telling how far the impact of your teaching may go; perhaps, to paraphrase the historian Henry Adams, even as far as eternity.

For Further Study

1. Reflect upon what you would like to do to awaken or reawaken aspects of your own inner genius. Look over your memories of peak learning experiences, activities that you are most passionate about in your current life, and things you'd like to do in the future if given the time and opportunity. Choose one or two of these and begin doing them. After some time, check in with colleagues who are engaged in their own process of genius exploration and share your experiences with them.

2. What are some experiences or materials that you've exposed your students to that have created special moments of joy, curiosity, playfulness, humor, or other qualities of genius? Look over the list of suggestions above and add your own ideas to them. Then try out one or two new possibilities with your class and share the responses with colleagues.

3. What parts of your current classroom setting show aspects of the genial climate described in this section? What other dimensions of a genial climate would you like to incorporate into your classroom? Choose one of these to focus on and spend some time exploring ways to integrate it into your program (e.g., experiment with a "test-free zone" in your classroom).

4. Describe each of your students in terms of one or more of the 12 qualities of genius described in this book. Then, add to this description aspects of one or more of the eight intelligences from the theory of multiple intelligences or another learning model that celebrates different ways of knowing and learning. Add other gifts, no matter how insignificant they may initially appear. Finally, put all these gifts together in a "genius description" for each of your students. Start with one or two students who have had particular difficulty functioning in school, and then work your way through the whole class over a period of weeks or months.

SELECTED RESOURCES

Awakening Your Child's Natural Genius: Enhancing Curiosity, Creativity, and Learning Ability, by Thomas Armstrong. New York: Tarcher/Putnam, 1991. Practical guide for parents and teachers that includes chapters on creative approaches to music, art, history, science, math, and reading.

Creative Education Foundation, 1050 Union Rd., Buffalo, NY 14224; 716-675-3181; fax: 716-675-3209. Publishes yearly catalog of resources on creativity for educators.

Experiences in Visual Thinking, by Robert H. McKim. Boston, MA: PSW Engineering, 1980. A marvelous collection of exercises for stimulating inventiveness and the imagination.

The Humor Project, 110 Spring St., Saratoga Springs, NY 12866; 800-225-0330. Has a mail-order service for resources on humor and creativity in the classroom, holds an annual international conference, publishes the periodical *Laughing Matters*, and holds workshops and seminars worldwide.

The Official Museum Directory, R. R. Bowker, P.O. Box 1001, Summit, NJ 07902-1001; 800-521-8110. A comprehensive listing of aquariums, arboretums, art museums, children's museums, history museums, planetariums, zoos, science and natural history museums, and more; listed by state.

Powers of Ten (film, 9 minutes), Charles and Ray Eames, producers, 1978. Pyramid Film and Video, Box 1048, 2801 Colorado Ave., Santa Monica, CA 90406; 800-421-2304. $125 (purchase); $60 (rental for educators). Takes the viewer on a journey into micro- and macro-worlds (from subatomic particles to the universe) by powers of ten. A brilliant film that evokes wonder in its viewers.

Workman Publishing Co., 708 Broadway, New York, NY 10003; 212-254-5900, 800-722-7202. Publishes books and materials for kids covering a wide range of areas from juggling and harmonica playing to science and history studies (including a do-it-yourself time capsule).

Zephyr Press, 3316 N. Chapel Ave., P.O. Box 66006-LA, Tucson, AZ 85728-6006. Publishes books and materials covering each of the eight intelligences in multiple intelligences theory.

REFERENCES

Adelman, H.S., V.M. MacDonald, P. Nelson, D.C. Smith, and L. Taylor. (March 1990). "Motivational Readiness and the Participation of Children with Learning and Behavioral Problems in Psychoeducational Decision Making." *Journal of Learning Disabilities* 23, 3: 171–176.

Alessandri, S.M., M.W. Sullivan, S. Imaizumi, and M. Lewis. (November 1993). "Learning and Emotional Responsivity in Cocaine-Exposed Infants." *Developmental Psychology* 29, 6: 989–997.

Allison, A.W. (1975). *The Norton Anthology of Poetry*. Rev. ed. New York: W.W. Norton.

Allport, G. (1954). *The Nature of Prejudice*. Cambridge, Mass.: Addison-Wesley.

Amabile, T. (1979). "Effects of External Evaluation on Artistic Creativity." *Journal of Personality and Social Psychology* 37, 2: 221–233.

Armstrong, T. (1984). *The Radiant Child*. Wheaton, Ill.: Theosophical Publishing House.

Armstrong, T. (1987a). "Describing Strengths in Children Identified as 'Learning Disabled' Using Howard Gardner's Theory of Multiple Intelligences as an Organizing Framework." *Dissertation Abstracts International* 48, 08A. (University Microfilms No. 87–25, 844).

Armstrong, T. (1987b). *In Their Own Way: Discovering and Encouraging Your Child's Personal Learning Style*. New York: Tarcher/Putnam.

Armstrong, T. (1988). "Learning Differences—Not Disabilities." *Principal* 68, 1: 34–36.

Armstrong, T. (1994). *Multiple Intelligences in the Classroom*. Alexandria, Va.: Association for Supervision and Curriculum Development.

Armstrong, T. (1995). *The Myth of the ADD Child: 50 Ways to Improve Your Child's Behavior and Attention Span Without Drugs, Labels, or Coercion*. New York: Dutton.

Armstrong, T. (October 18, 1995). "ADD as a Social Invention." *Education Week*, p. 40.

Armstrong, T. (1996a). "ADD: Does It Really Exist?" *Phi Delta Kappan* 77, 6: 424–428.

Armstrong, T. (1996b). "A Holistic Approach to Attention Deficit Disorder." *Educational Leadership*, 53, 5: 34–36.

Armstrong, T. (1997). *Multiple Intelligences: Discovering the Giftedness in All* (videotape). Port Chester, N.Y.: National Professional Resources.

Ashton-Warner, S. (1986). *Teacher*. New York: Simon and Schuster.

Begley, S. (June 2, 1986). "Going with the Flow." *Newsweek*, pp. 68–69.

Bellanca, J., C. Chapman, and E. Swartz. (1994). *Multiple Assessments for Multiple Intelligences*. Palatine, Ill.: IRI/Skylight Publishing.

Bickerton, D. (July 1982). "Creole Languages." *Scientific American*, pp. 116–122.

Blakeslee, S. (April 17, 1997). "Studies Show Talking with Infants Shapes Basis of Ability to Think." *The New York Times*, p. A14.

Blakeslee, S. (August 1, 1997). "Study Finds That Baby Talk Means More Than a Coo." *The New York Times*, p. A14.

Bloom, B., ed. (1985). *Developing Talent in Young People*. New York: Ballantine Books.

Bradley, A. (November 22, 1995). "What Price Success? Honored Teachers Sometimes Face Scorn, Ridicule of Colleagues." *Education Week*, pp. 1, 8–9.

Bradshaw, J. (1988). *Healing the Shame That Binds You*. Deerfield Beach, Fla: Health Communications.

Brod, C. (1984). *TechnoStress: The Human Cost of the Computer Revolution*. Reading, Mass.: Addison-Wesley.

Bruetsch, A. (1995). *Multiple Intelligences Lesson Plan Book*. Tucson, Ariz.: Zephyr Press.

Campbell, L., B. Campbell, and D. Dickinson. (1996). *Teaching and Learning Through Multiple Intelligences*. Needham Heights, Mass.: Allyn and Bacon.

Canfield, J., and H.C. Wells. (1976). *100 Ways to Enhance Self-Concept in the Classroom*. Englewood Cliffs, N.J.: Prentice-Hall.

Carini, P. (1982). *The School Lives of Seven Children: A Five Year Study*. Grand Forks, N.D.: University of North Dakota.

Casals, P. (April 1983). "Joys and Sorrows: Reflections by Pablo Casals." *On the Beam* III, 4:101.

Chamberlain, D.B. (1988). *Babies Remember Birth*. New York: Tarcher/Putnam.

Chernoff, J.M. (1979). "Music-making Children of Africa." *Natural History* 88, 6: 68–75.

Chukovskii, K. (1963). *From Two to Five*. Berkeley, Calif.: University of California Press.

Clark, R.W. (1984). *Einstein: The Life and Times*. New York: Avon.

Cole, K.C. (November 30, 1988). "Play, by Definition, Suspends the Rules." *The New York Times*, p. C16.

Coles, G. (1987). *The Learning Mystique: A Critical Look at "Learning Disabilities."* New York: Pantheon.

Coles, R. (1967). *Children of Crisis*. Boston: Little Brown.

Coles, R. (1986a). *The Moral Life of Children*. Boston: Atlantic Monthly Press.

Coles, R. (1986b). *The Political Life of Children*. Boston: Atlantic Monthly Press.

Coles, R. (1990). *The Spiritual Life of Children*. Boston: Houghton Mifflin.

Compact Oxford English Dictionary, The. (1991). 2nd ed. Oxford, England: Clarendon Press.

Comstock, G., and H. Paik. (1991). *Television and the American Child*. San Diego: Academic Press.

Cousins, N. (1979). *Anatomy of an Illness as Perceived by the Patient*. New York: W.W. Norton.

Cowan, M. (1979). "The Development of the Brain." In *The Brain* (a *Scientific American* book). New York: W.H. Freeman and Co.

Cramond, B. (1994). "Attention-Deficit Hyperactivity Disorder and Creativity: What Is the Connection?" *Journal of Creative Behavior* 28, 2: 193–210.

Csikszentmihalyi, M. (1990). *Flow: The Psychology of Optimal Experience*. New York: Harper Collins.

Csikszentmihalyi, M., K. Rathunde, and S. Whalen. (1993). *Talented Teenagers: The Roots of Success and Failure*. New York: Cambridge University Press.

Cuffaro, H. (Summer 1984). "Microcomputers in Education: Why Is Earlier Better?" *Teachers College Record* 85, 4: 559–568.

Davidson, R.J. (1992). "Emotion and Affective Style: Hemispheric Substrates." *Psychological Science* 3, 1: 39–43.

Davidson, R.J. (1994). "Asymmetric Brain Function, Affective Style, and Psychopathology: The Role of Early Experience and Plasticity, Sensitive Periods, and Psychopathology." *Development and Psychopathology* 6, 4: 741–758.

Davy, J. (Summer 1984). "Mindstorms in the Lamplight." *Teachers College Record* 85, 4: 549–558.

Diamond, M.C. (1988). *Enriching Heredity: The Impact of the Environment on the Anatomy of the Brain*. New York: The Free Press.

Doman, G. (1964). *How to Teach Your Baby to Read*. New York: Random House.

Dunn, R., and K. Dunn. (1978). *Teaching Students Through Their Individual Learning Styles*. Reston, Va.: Reston Publishing Co.

Egan, K. (1992). *Imagination in Teaching and Learning: The Middle School Years*. Chicago: University of Chicago Press.

Ekman, P., and R.J. Davidson. (1993). "Voluntary Smiling Changes Regional Brain Activity." *Psychological Science* 4, 5: 342–345.

Elkind, D. (1981). *The Hurried Child: Growing Up Too Fast Too Soon*. Reading, Mass.: Addison-Wesley.

Elkind, D. (1984). *All Grown Up and No Place to Go: Teenagers in Crisis*. Reading, Mass.: Addison-Wesley.

Feldman, D. (1980). *Beyond Universals in Cognitive Development*. Norwood, N.J.: Ablex.

Fogarty, R., and J. Stoehr. (1995). *Integrating Curricula with Multiple Intelligences*. Palatine, Ill.: IRI/Skylight Publishing.

Foster, G.G., C.R. Schmidt, and D. Sabatino. (1976). "Teacher Expectancies and the Label Learning Disabilities." *Journal of Learning Disabilities* 9, 2: 111–114.

Froebel, F. (1887). *The Education of Man*. New York: D. Appleton and Company.

Gallas, K. (1994). *The Languages of Learning: How Children Talk, Write, Dance, Draw, and Sing Their Understanding of The World*. New York: Teachers College Press.

Gardner, H. (December 1981). "Do Babies Sing a Universal Song?" *Psychology Today*, pp. 70–76.

Gardner, H. (1983). *Frames of Mind: The Theory of Multiple Intelligences*. New York: Basic Books.

Gardner, H. (1993a). *Multiple Intelligences: The Theory in Practice*. New York: Basic Books.

Gardner, H. (1993b). *Creating Minds*. New York: Basic Books.

Gardner, H. (1995). *How Are Kids Smart?: Multiple Intelligences in the Classroom* (videotape). Port Chester, N.Y.: National Professional Resources.

Gardner, H. (1996). "Are There Additional Intelligences? The Case for Naturalist, Spiritual, and Existential Intelligences." In *Education, Information, and Transformation*, edited by J. Kane. Englewood Cliffs, N.J.: Prentice-Hall.

Getzels, J.W., and P.W. Jackson. (1962). *Creativity and Intelligence: Explorations with Gifted Students*. London: Wiley.

Ghiselin, B., ed. (1955). *The Creative Process*. New York: Mentor.

Ginsburg, H., and S. Opper. (1969). *Piaget's Theory of Intellectual Development*. Englewood Cliffs, N.J.: Prentice Hall.

Goleman, D. (1995). *Emotional Intelligence: Why It Can Matter More Than I.Q.* New York: Bantam.

Goodlad, J.I. (1984). *A Place Called School*. New York: McGraw-Hill.

Gould, S.J. (1977). "The Child as Man's Real Father." In *Ever Since Darwin: Reflections in Natural History*. New York: W.W. Norton.

Gowan, J.C., G.D. Demos, and E.P. Torrance. (1967). *Creativity: Its Educational Implications*. New York: J. Wiley.

Greene, M. (1995). "Art and Imagination: Reclaiming the Sense of Possibility." *Phi Delta Kappan* 76, 5: 378–382.

Guilford, J.P. (1977). *Way Beyond the IQ*. Buffalo, N.Y.: Creative Education Foundation.

Haggerty, B. (1995). *Nurturing Intelligences: A Guide to Multiple Intelligences Theory and Teaching*. Menlo Park, Calif.: Addison-Wesley.

Harman, W., and H. Rheingold. (1984). *Higher Creativity: Liberating the Unconscious for Breakthrough Insights*. New York: Tarcher/Putnam.

Harwood, A.C. (1958). *The Recovery of Man in Childhood*. London: Hodder and Stoughton.

Healy, J. (1990). *Endangered Minds: Why Children Don't Think and What We Can Do About It*. New York: Simon and Schuster.

Hebert, P.J. (April 11–14, 1991). "Humor in the Classroom: Theories, Functions, and Guidelines." Paper presented at the annual meeting of the Central States Communication Association, Chicago, Ill. (ERIC ED336769).

Holt, J. (1970). *How Children Fail*. New York: Dell.

Houston, J. (1982). *The Possible Human: A Course in Enhancing Your Physical, Mental, and Creative Abilities*. New York: Tarcher/Putnam.

Huesmann, L.R., and L.D. Eron, eds. (1986). *Television and the Aggressive Child: A Cross-National Comparison*. Hillsdale, N.J.: Lawrence Erlbaum.

Hughes, B., H.J. Sullivan, and M.L. Mosley. (March/April 1985). "Evaluation, Task Difficulty, and Continuing Motivation." *Journal of Educational Research* 78, 4: 210–215.

Hunter, E. (1993). "Fostering Creativity: Ensuring Quality in Education." *NASSP Bulletin* 77, 555: 101–109.

Israel, E. (1995). "Developing High School Students' Creativity by Teaching Them to Take Risks and Defer Judgment." Ed.D. practicum, Nova Southeastern University (ERIC ED387788).

Jersild, A. (1955). *When Teachers Face Themselves*. New York: Teachers College Press.

John-Steiner, V. (1985). *Notebooks of the Mind: Explorations of Thinking*. New York: Harper and Row.

Jung, C. (1963). *Memories, Dreams, Reflections*. New York: Vintage.

Kirschenbaum, H., R. Napier, and S.B. Simon. (1971). *Wad-ja-get? The Grading Game in American Education*. New York: Hart.

Kline, P. (1988). *The Everyday Genius: Restoring Children's Natural Joy of Learning—and Yours Too*. Arlington, Va.: Great Ocean.

Koch, K. (1970). *Wishes, Lies, and Dreams: Teaching Children to Write Poetry*. New York: Vintage.

Kohn, A. (1993). *Punished by Rewards: The Trouble With Gold Stars, Incentive Plans, A's, Praise, and Other Bribes*. Boston: Houghton Mifflin.

Kozol, J. (1991). *Savage Inequalities: Children in America's Schools*. New York: Crown.

Kozol, J. (1995). *Amazing Grace: The Lives of Children and the Conscience of a Nation*. New York: Crown.

Krippner, S. (Autumn 1967). "The Ten Commandments That Block Creativity." *Gifted Child Quarterly* XI, 2: 144–156.

Lash, J.P. (1980). *Helen and Teacher: The Story of Helen Keller and Anne Sullivan Macy*. New York: Delacorte.

Lazear, D. (1991). *Seven Ways of Teaching: The Artistry of Teaching with Multiple Intelligences*. Palatine, Ill.: Skylight Publishing.

Leonard, G. (1968). *Education and Ecstasy*. New York: Delacorte Press.

Lipman, M., A.M. Sharp, and F.S. Oscanyan. (1980). *Philosophy in the Classroom.* Philadelphia: Temple University Press.

Litterst, J.H., and A. Bassey. (1993). "Developing Classroom Imagination: Shaping and Energizing a Suitable Climate for Growth, Discovery, and Vision." *Journal of Creative Behavior* 27, 1: 270–282.

Lorie, P. (1989). *Wonder Child: Rediscovering the Magical World of Innocence and Joy Within Ourselves and Our Children.* New York: Simon and Schuster.

Mander, J. (1978). *Four Arguments for the Elimination of Television.* New York: Morrow/ Quill.

Mann, D. (1996). "Serious Play." *Teachers College Record* 97, 3: 116–169.

Margulies, N. (1995). *The Magic 7: Tools for Building Your Multiple Intelligences.* Tucson, Ariz.: Zephyr Press.

Maslow, A. (1954). *Motivation and Personality.* New York: Harper and Row.

Matthews, G.B. (1980). *Philosophy and the Young Child.* Cambridge, Mass.: Harvard University Press.

Matthews, G.B. (1984). *Dialogues with Children.* Cambridge, Mass.: Harvard University Press.

Matthews, G.B. (1994). *The Philosophy of Childhood.* Cambridge, Mass.: Harvard University Press.

McCarthy, B. (1987). *The 4Mat System: Teaching to Learning Styles with Right/Left Mode Techniques.* Barrington, Ill.: Excel.

McKim, R. (1980). *Experiences in Visual Thinking.* Boston: PWS/Wadsworth.

Mearns, H. (1958). *Creative Power: The Education of Youth in Creative Arts.* New York: Dover.

Montagu, A. (1983). *Growing Young.* New York: McGraw-Hill.

Montessori, M. (1973). *The Secret of Childhood.* New York: Ballantine Books.

Murray, B. (April 1997). "Is the Internet Feeding Junk to Students?" *APA Monitor* (American Psychological Association), p. 50.

Natale, J.A. (October 1995). "Making Smart Cool." *Executive Educator* 17, 10: 20–24.

New Encyclopaedia Britannica, The. (1980). Chicago, Ill.: Encyclopaedia Britannica, Inc.

Noble, E. (1993). *Primal Connections: How Our Experiences from Conception to Birth Influence Our Emotions, Behavior, and Health.* New York: Simon and Schuster.

Oakes, J. (1985). *Keeping Track: How Schools Structure Inequality.* New Haven, Conn.: Yale University Press.

Oakes, J., and M. Lipton. (1990). *Making the Best of Schools: A Handbook for Parents, Teachers, and Policymakers.* New Haven, Conn.: Yale University Press.

O'Brien, G. (February 6, 1997). "The Ghost at the Feast." *The New York Review of Books* XLIV, 2: p. 13.

Ostrander, S., and L. Schroeder. (1979). *Superlearning.* New York: Delta.

Piaget, J. (1952). *The Origins of Intelligence in Children*. New York: International University Press.

Piaget, J. (1975). *The Child's Conception of the World*. Totowa, N.J.: Littlefield, Adams and Co.

Pipher, M. (1995). *Reviving Ophelia: Saving the Selves of Adolescent Girls*. New York: Ballantine.

Provenzo, E.F., and A. Brett. (1983). *The Complete Block Book*. Syracuse, N.Y.: Syracuse University Press.

Rejskind, F.G. (1982). "Autonomy and Creativity in Children." *The Journal of Creative Behavior* 16, 1: 58–67.

Renzulli, J.S. (1986). "The Three-Ring Conception of Gifted-ness: A Developmental Model for Creative Productivity." In *Conceptions of Giftedness*, edited by R.J. Sternberg and J.E. Davidson. New York: Cambridge University Press.

Robinson, E. (1983). *The Original Vision*. New York: The Seabury Press.

Rosenthal, R., and L. Jacobsen. (1968). *Pygmalion in the Classroom: Teacher Expectations and Pupils' Intellectual Development*. New York: Holt, Rinehart and Winston.

Rosenthal, R., and D.B. Rubin. (1978). "Interpersonal Expectancy Effects: The First 345 Studies." *The Behavioral and Brain Sciences* 3: 377–415.

Rosensweig, M., E.L. Bennett, and M.C. Diamond. (February 1972). "Brain Changes in Response to Experience." *Scientific American* 226, 2: 22–29.

Rutter, M. (1985). "Family and School Influences on Cognitive Development." *Journal of Child Psychology and Psychiatry* 26, 5: 683–704.

Samples, B. (1976). *The Metaphoric Mind: A Celebration of Creative Consciousness*. Reading, Mass.: Addison-Wesley.

Satir, V. (1988). *The New Peoplemaking*. Mountain View, Calif.: Science and Behavior Books.

Shearer, B. (1996). *The MIDAS (Multiple Intelligences Developmental Assessment Scales): A Guide to Assessment and Education for the Multiple Intelligences*. Columbus, Ohio: Greyden Press.

Silverstein, S. (1980). *The Child Is Superior to the Man*. Hicksville, N.Y.: Exposition Press.

Simon, S.B., and J.A. Bellanca, eds. (1976). *Degrading the Grading Myths: A Primer of Alternatives to Grades and Marks*. Washington, D.C.: Association for Supervision and Curriculum Development.

Singer, J.L. (1973). *The Child's World of Make-Believe: Experimental Studies of Imaginative Play*. New York: Academic Press.

Singer, J.L., and D.G. Singer. (1981). *Television, Imagination, and Aggression: A Study of Preschoolers*. Hillsdale, N.J.: L. Erlbaum.

Smith, F. (1986). *Insult to Intelligence: The Bureaucratic Invasion of Our Classrooms*. New York: Arbor House.

Sornson, R., and J. Scott. (1997). *Teaching and Joy*. Alexandria, Va.: Association for Supervision and Curriculum Development.

Steiner, R. (1982). *The Kingdom of Childhood*. London: Rudolf Steiner Press.

Sternberg, R.J. (1988). *The Triarchic Mind: A New Theory of Human Intelligence*. New York: Penguin Books.

Sutton-Smith, B. (1986). *Toys as Culture*. New York: Gardner Press.

Sylwester, R. (1995). *A Celebration of Neurons: An Educator's Guide to the Brain*. Alexandria, Va.: Association for Supervision and Curriculum Development.

Tarver, S.G., P.S. Ellsworth, and D.J. Rounds. (Summer 1980). "Figural and Verbal Creativity in Learning Disabled and Nondisabled Children." *Learning Disability Quarterly* 3: 11–18.

Taylor, C.W. (December 1968). "Be Talent Developers as Well as Knowledge Dispensers." *Today's Education*, pp. 67–69.

Teele, S. (1992). *The Teele Inventory for Multiple Intelligences (TIMI)*. Redlands, Calif.: Sue Teele and Associates.

Torrance, E.P. (1962). *Guiding Creative Talent*. Englewood Cliffs, N.J.: Prentice-Hall.

Tyson-Bernstein, H. (1988). *A Conspiracy of Good Intentions: America's Textbook Fiasco*. Washington, D.C.: Council for Basic Education.

Tyson, H., and A. Woodward. (November 1989). "Why Students Aren't Learning Very Much from Textbooks." *Educational Leadership* 47: 14–17.

Van de Carr, F.R. (1992). *Prenatal Classroom: A Parents' Guide for Teaching Your Baby in the Womb*. Atlanta, Ga.: Humanics Learning.

Verny, T. (1981). *The Secret Life of the Unborn Child*. New York: Delta.

Walters, J., and H. Gardner. (1986). "The Crystallizing Experience: Discovery of an Intellectual Gift." In *Conceptions of Giftedness*, edited by R. Sternberg and J. Davidson. New York: Cambridge University Press.

Weinreich-Haste, H. (1985). "The Varieties of Intelligence—An Interview with Howard Gardner." *New Ideas in Psychology* 3, 1: 48.

Werner, H. (1948). *Comparative Psychology of Mental Development*. New York: International Universities Press.

West, T.G. (1991). *In the Mind's Eye: Visual Thinkers, Gifted People with Learning Difficulties, Computer Images, and the Ironies of Creativity*. Buffalo, N.Y.: Prometheus Books.

Wheelock, A. (1992). *Crossing the Tracks: How "Untracking" Can Save America's Schools*. New York: The New Press.

Whitehead, A.N. (1932). *The Aims of Education and Other Essays*. London: Williams and Norgate Ltd.

Wickes, F.G. (1966). *The Inner World of Childhood*. New York: Mentor.

Wright, L.B., and V.A. LaMar, eds. (1964). *The Two Gentlemen of Verona by William Shakespeare*. New York: Washington Square Press.

Yarborough, B.H., and R.A. Johnson. (April 1980). "Research That Questions the Traditional Elementary School Marking System." *Phi Delta Kappan* 61, 8: 527–528.

Zentall, S.S. (1988). "Production Deficiencies in Elicited Language but Not in the Spontaneous Verbalizations of Hyperactive Children." *Journal of Abnormal Child Psychology* 16, 6: 657–673.

Zipes, J., ed. (1991). *Arabian Nights: The Marvels and Wonders of the Thousand and One Nights*. New York: Signet.

About the Author

Thomas Armstrong, Ph.D., is the author of eight books, including *Multiple Intelligences in the Classroom*, *In Their Own Way*, *Awakening Your Child's Natural Genius*, *7 Kinds of Smart*, and *The Myth of the ADD Child*. He can be reached by mail at P.O. Box 548, Cloverdale, CA 95425, by phone at 707-894-4646, or by fax at 707-894-4474.